2011

Dominique Bouchait
Meilleur Ouvrier De Fran...
Classe Fromager

To my parents, Yvonne and Robert. You started the ball rolling,
and I have done my best to keep it going.
I want to turn your heritage into something beautiful that
we can all be proud of passing on to my son, Antoine.

FROMAGES

AN EXPERT'S GUIDE TO FRENCH CHEESE

DOMINIQUE
BOUCHAIT

RIZZOLI
NEW YORK

New York · Paris · London · Milan

Summary

RECIPES

BEING A CHEESEMONGER
by Dominique Bouchait

At home, my grandmother, Antoinette, did the cooking while my parents, Yvonne and Robert, taught me the essential things in life. From a young age, I learned the smell and taste of good cheeses. I grew up in Montréjeau at the foot of the Pyrenees Mountains in southwestern France, where my family had a delicatessen selling cheese. During my vacations, from the age of eleven, I would help cure ham, grind pepper and coffee, fill wine crates, and load trucks. I was not allowed to touch the cheese: it was far too fragile and precious, and not suitable for children to handle. The special treatment cheese enjoyed could have piqued my curiosity and interest, but ornithology was my great passion. I had already decided what I wanted to become when I grew up: an ornithologist!

Time went by, and while my passion for birdlife continued, my parents gradually managed to get me interested in their profession. In the 1970s, refrigerated transport technology improved, which meant it was possible to expand to the far-flung reaches of France to discover regional specialties, usually confined to their local area. It meant my parents' role had to change. To survive, suddenly they were forced to offer a more varied range of products. In the Southwest, demand for northern cheeses—real Camembert from Normandy, Comté from the east, Brie de Meaux from outside Paris—soared. So they had to venture to new pastures. The first market stand for their cheese retail business opened on Labor Day, May 1, 1976. Ten years later I joined the adventure. Today, although far from my childhood dreams, my current profession is so absorbing that it has become a passion in its own right.

The French Cheesemonger's Profession

I have been a cheesemonger since the age of twenty and I received the prestigious Meilleur Ouvrier de France (MOF) award at the age of forty-five, a nationally recognized award for the finest craftsmen in their trade. Gradually, I have perfected my craft to become an "artisan." Artisan status in France is awarded to people who respect traditional values in their profession. Thanks to the work of Carole Delga, Philippe Olivier, Stéphane Vergne, and David Bazergue, this status was accorded to the cheesemonger profession in 2015.

Facing page: A family of producers around their cheese. The grandmother is one hundred. She has tasted a few cheeses in her time.

As Joël Robuchon said, "You're not born Meilleur Ouvrier de France, you become it." It is a heavy responsibility but brings a great sense of honor. From the moment I received the award I had to offer the best of myself, at any moment and with everybody. I have to live up to my name, in both appearance and skills. I have to ask searching questions of myself and seek constant self-improvement, not in a commercial sense but in terms of quality: Everything I do has to strive for excellence, and not only in the taste of my products, which is a more subjective criterion. Being a Meilleur Ouvrier de France cheesemonger means knowing how to create the best cheeses as they should be made. This distinction has also changed my way of working. If I clean my knives five times a day, it is because this search for excellence also applies to hygiene. In presentation every aspect has to be perfect; the way we use every inch of space has to be impeccable; every detail has to be perfect; the public should never get to see anything unacceptable, like a dirty knife or a messy workstation. People expect perfection and expect our presentation to be top-notch. So every day I recall Victor Hugo's phrase: "Form is content that has risen to the surface."

Why I Wrote This Book

I wanted to write this book as a tribute to all our wonderful cheeses, of course, but also for my friends and family, especially my parents who embarked on the profession through economic necessity and who gave me the desire to create a business in the cheese world. They also passed along core values and principles such as "work better to live better." I hope my parents would have been proud of this book.

Becoming Meilleur Ouvrier de France

The aim of the Meilleurs Ouvriers de France movement is: "To provide a federation for France's most specialized artisans to promote French savoir faire and excellence and pass it on to younger generations." Created in 1929 by a cabinetmaker, René Petit, today the association has eighteen hundred members representing roughly two hundred trades. A Meilleur Ouvrier de France (MOF) is recognized at the national level by both industry peers and clients. For experienced workers it represents the summit of their career, a lifetime achievement award; for younger artisans it provides a magnificent springboard for starting out. The competition takes place every three or four years in several stages to select the best candidates. The competition I won in 2011 involved:

• Testing specialist knowledge of products and the sector: technology, history, terroir, milk cow species, cheese manufacture, origin labeling (AOP), etc;

• Taste tests and the presentation of a selection of cheeses to demonstrate organoleptic command, ripeness recognition, and ability to talk about cheese, its flavors, textures, and manufacture;

• Management, cutting, and packaging: the preparation of a balanced cheese platter;

• Cheese and cuisine: the preparation of a cheese-based specialty in the presence of a professional jury;

• Creation of a cheese buffet, or exceptional presentation.

The Meilleur Ouvrier de France's Influence on My Life

The day I won the competition, others' views of me changed. Everywhere. Being Meilleur Ouvrier de France gave me peer recognition and respect from clients and cheese specialists in France and abroad, especially in Asia, where the award is highly respected.

Becoming Meilleur Ouvrier de France meant I could expand my team: in four years, we grew from eleven to thirty-nine employees. Before I had difficulty recruiting personnel for such an itinerant, market-based trade; today I get requests from young people starting out who want to have their cheesemonger apprenticeship with me. The award provides an important reference, and is a guarantee of quality and skill level. My suppliers, especially, sense the exacting nature of the role. There is no way I can sell cheeses with too much salt, or cheeses that do not comply with regulations. Quality comes first, above all other economic or logistic criteria. Suppliers are well aware of this.

Going International

Becoming Meilleur Ouvrier de France has helped me branch out internationally. It opened my eyes to the Austrian market, even if I had already worked abroad. At the age of thirty-eight, I felt my daily market-sales routine needed to be changed. So I left to work with professional cheese producers: Laurent Dubois, Marie Quatrehomme, Martine Dubois, Nicole Barthélémy, the Odéon group, Philippe Olivier, Cyrille Lorho, Bernard Mure-Ravaud, Philippe Marchand, and Michelle Mimi Thieullent, among many others. Thanks to them, I developed my savoir faire and acquired new skill sets. Then I went to Holland to learn with René Koelman, to Belgium with Michel Van Tricht, to Japan with Mrs. Hisada, to Sweden with Androuet, and to Denmark with Catherine Fogel. Observing all these exceptional cheesemakers and the way they work so differently broadened my mind. In France, we dare not stray from tradition. Abroad, people invent new ideas, reinvent old ideas, or suggest new tweaks to old tricks whether in sales, presentation, or supports. Demand for my work increased in France but also abroad. People like Bernard Leprince, the chief chef at Frères Blanc brasseries, and Guillaume Gomez, the chef for the French president at Élysée Palace, opened up prestigious doors for me. Most of my services involved presentations and demonstrations. Today these still take up two-thirds of my time. I recently joined the Académie Culinaire de France, and am regularly called upon for high-end services, like a hunting feast at Paul Bocuse's restaurant in Lyon, in late 2015.

My Team

Becoming Meilleur Ouvrier de France strengthened team spirit. Everyone who I worked with helped me. Entering the competition was a challenge for all of us, and I am particularly grateful to Christiane Duplan and Corine Boucheron who, in addition to encouraging me to take part, admirably assisted Jennifer Dumoret and Sylvie Abadie, who won the Gold Lyre for the cheese platter competition.

An artisan cheesemonger cannot just settle for buying and selling cheese, they also have to bring their own special, personal touch to the trade and demonstrate a deep reverence for cutting, presentation, and packaging. Respecting cheese, above all, means respecting, promoting, and nurturing the whole manufacturing process, from the animal that provides the milk to the consumer who buys and eats the cheese. A good artisan knows how to get the best out of their cheeses.

Our "Cheese Bar"

I wanted to show that a cheesemonger is an artisan who does more than simply ripen cheese. Ripening is only a small part of their skill set. They also know how to create a context for tasting. In my cheese bar, we invite cheese lovers to discover different ways of tasting cheese by preparing a variety of homemade recipes before their eyes—some original, some classics—with cheese as the main ingredient, of course!

All the professionals in the bar are top-notch cheesemongers and explain their creations, choices, and pairings with customers. It becomes a fun and friendly focal point for discussion and trying things out. The bar represents a different way to look at my profession. When you feel that passion for something, you want to share it.

Why We Focus on AOP Cheeses

The Appelation d'Origine Protégé (AOP) is a label that guarantees cheeses come from a particular region and are manufactured according to the correct methods and standards. I did not want to write a dictionary or encyclopedia of cheeses, but I did want to talk about my profession and France's finest cheeses. Deciding whether a cheese is good is a subjective process. So I decided to focus on AOP cheeses. My approach makes sense and expresses a militant position: it makes sense because the AOP label guarantees quality and authenticity; it is militant because today there is only one thing that can save the milk industry—the production of AOP-quality milk! Applying a verified organoleptic series of regulations guarantees quality for the cheese industry. I am not saying that only AOP cheeses are good. There are many delicious cheeses in France and around the world that are not AOP cheeses. The best way to find them is to ask dedicated professionals and artisan cheesemongers.

Qualities of a Good Cheesemonger

A good cheesemonger is readily recognizable by the line outside their store or by their stand at markets. But not only that. Every detail counts, from their storefront (or truck) to the way they present their cheese. Then there are hygiene issues; the tools used and the service provided are crucial. The artisan's cheese expertise is invaluable, too, from the advice they give to the packaging—the quality of the wrapping paper, the bag used, etc. Everything counts. Passionate about their profession, a good cheesemonger is always eager to share their knowledge, with customers and employees alike. They are meticulous in their selection of cheeses and respect their products. They know how to say "no" when a cheese is unsuitable, in the interests of both customers and the cheese itself.

Qualities of a Good Customer

There is no definition of a good customer. Obviously, we are fond of our loyal customers; they give us the conviction and professional conscience we need in our daily work. We do get the occasional difficult customer—always memorable, but fortunately rare. Our favorite customers share moments of their lives with us—weddings, birthdays, communions, family celebrations, and dinners among friends. That is when we get to genuinely exercise our art, composing platters and buffets for festive occasions. It is a great joy of the trade.

Cheese and Gastronomy

Since 2010, French gastronomy has been listed on the UNESCO Intangible Heritage list, which states: "A French gastronomic meal has to respect a specific format: it should begin with an aperitif and end with a digestif, with at least four dishes in between: a starter, fish and/or meat with vegetables, cheese, and dessert."

Above Left: Some of the team at the Mont-Royal cheese store. *Above Right:* A winter squash velouté made with the local blue cheese, César Régalis, created at the bar.

ALL ABOUT CHEESE

WHAT IS CHEESE?
Presentation, History, and Origins

In France, cheese is as emblematic as the beret, baguette, striped T-shirt, and moustache. Cheese is one of the jewels in the French gastronomic crown. It is not, however, specifically French. It has no specific home. The thousands of varieties to be found around the world speak of an ancient and diverse history and multiple origins. Why does cheese have such a hallowed status on the French dinner table? What differentiates French cheese from cheese elsewhere in the world? Where does cheese come from? And who first had the idea to make it?

The Word "Cheese"

"Cheese" refers to a product created from the curds of milk. The milk may be full cream or skim. The production process may simply use the cream or butterfat, alone or in a coagulated mixture, whole or in part, before the product is drained and the whey partially eliminated.

Some cheeses have Appellation d'Origine Protégée status (AOP), an official sign of quality, which guarantees their regional provenance, the nature of their terroir, the milk used, and the manufacturing process deployed from curdling the milk to ripening the cheese.

> *Did you know?*
>
> Many will be familiar with "fake cheeses" that have the texture and appearance of Cheddar, mozzarella, and Emmental, but are actually created using the chemicals E410, E412, E417, and E407. These synthetic cheeses incorporate a combination of starches and thickening agents to create a product with a similar texture to cheese but without containing a single ounce of dairy product.
>
> These are the cheeses we find sprinkled on pizzas and seeping out of hamburgers. The synthetic form contains zero lactose or animal proteins (which some consumers find to be an advantage) but, as a result, zero nutritional value as well. And their taste? I shall let you be the judge.

The First Cheeses

According to legend, an Arab shepherd carrying a sheep's-belly flask full of milk, had to walk home beneath the desert sun. When he got home he realized his milk had solidified: the milk had curdled and cheese was born.

Other stories abound and whoever "invented" cheese or wherever it "originated" is still a mystery. In Europe, historians have traced major advances in cheese production to the expansion of the Roman Empire. It was during this period that the surfaces of unripe cheeses were salted for the first time to help form rinds and enhance preservation. The sacking of Rome by the Visigoths is said to have brought further progress in cheese manufacture—especially in Cantabria, Galicia, and the Pyrenees.

From archaeological excavations we have discovered that mankind has been making cheese ever since we started raising livestock—ten thousand years ago, at least. Its invention very possibly stemmed from a desire to preserve milk, a precious foodstuff.

The Oldest Cheeses

In Ancient Rome, the ancestors of Cantal and Roquefort today were exported from Gaul. The Romans used small cheese strainers known as *faisselles* to drain the curds, eliminating most of the whey and preserving as many milk solids as possible. In Toulouse, in the first century CE, ewe's cheeses from the Pyrenees were sold in markets. It was in the Middle Ages that a great many of today's French cheeses appeared. Especially productive were monks who had to comply with Lent, a fasting period of forty days during which all meat was forbidden and only one meal was allowed at the end of the day. Confined to a cheese-based diet, they developed production techniques to create more varied, flavorful varieties, some of which have survived today.

❖ *Hard cheeses like Parmesan, Cheddar, Comté, and Emmental are the product of Darwinian cheese evolution. They started as fresh cheeses before becoming soft cheeses with natural rinds; then blue cheese techniques were developed. Hard cheeses first made their appearance in about the thirteenth century, when the creation of* fruitières*, or cheese dairies (see page 116), appeared. The dairies pooled milk from several local cheese producers enabling larger-sized cheeses to be produced.*

THE CHEESE FAMILIES:
THE FORTY-FIVE AOP CHEESES

FRESH CHEESES

Brocciu, or Brocciu Corse

SOFT CHEESES WITH NATURAL RINDS

Chabichou du Poitou - Charolais - Chavignol, or Crottin de Chavignol - Mâconnais - Pélardon
Picodon - Picodon Dieulefit - Pouligny-Saint-Pierre - Rigotte de Condrieu - Rocamadour
Sainte-Maure-de-Touraine - Selles-sur-Cher - Valençay

SOFT CHEESES WITH WASHED RINDS

Époisses - Langres - Livarot - Maroilles - Mont d'Or, or Vacherin du Haut-Doubs
Munster or Munster-Géromé – Pont l'Evêque

SOFT CHEESES WITH BLOOMY RINDS

Banon - Brie de Meaux - Brie de Melun - Camembert de Normandie
Chaource - Neufchâtel

COOKED PRESSED CHEESES

Beaufort - Comté

SEMI-COOKED PRESSED CHEESES

Abondance

UNCOOKED PRESSED CHEESES

Cantal - Chevrotin - Laguiole - Morbier - Ossau-iraty - Reblochon de Savoie
Saint-Nectaire - Salers - Tome des Bauges

BLUE-VEINED CHEESES

Bleu d'Auvergne - Bleu de Gex Haut-Jura, or Bleu de Septmoncel - Bleu des Causses
Bleu du Vercors-Sassenage - Fourme d'Ambert - Fourme de Montbrison - Roquefort

Why Humans Began Making Cheese

We have long known that milk is highly nutritious. In the Neolithic period, when people started domesticating livestock, mankind was already drawing on milk's great potential. Curdling it and turning it into cheese was the only way to preserve a fragile foodstuff. From that point on, people started inventing ever more sophisticated agricultural means in order to obtain preservable foods and to survive the harsh winters ahead: cheese was humanity's first preserve, it is said, as human beings gradually learned to fill their larders.

At first, cheese was considered to be second best to meat, a paltry replacement on lean days. Only later did it attain its own special status before becoming a national treasure in France.

The Number of Cheeses

There is no official international cheese classification and there is no catalog of world cheeses, so there is no way of knowing how many cheeses there are. Over one thousand, for sure, but between tradition and constant innovation, new cheeses appear and old ones disappear from week to week. Cheese is also a victim of fashion.

Today in Europe there are over 165 AOP-labeled cheeses, butters, or creams—the products that comply with the correct quality criteria: their origins are verified; they use milk from the specified breed of livestock (whether cow, goat, ewe, or buffalo); they are produced by a recognized and qualified cheesemaker; and their production techniques follow traditional processes and adhere to a clear list of regulations. France has fifty such products, including forty-five cheeses, guaranteeing the consumer flavorful, aroma-specific products produced in an authentic way.

Each AOP cheese is evaluated several times a year to make sure it conforms to requirements. The manufacturing processes are observed and the cheese is subjected to a blind tasting by an independent certification body endorsed by the body governing all regional product labeling, the Institut National des Appellations d'Origine (INAO).

Preceding page: A "household cheese," the Barousse in Sost from the Pyrenees (Department 65).

Brie de Meaux

Bleu du Vercors-Sassenage

Époisses

Livarot

Pont-l'évêque

Selles-sur-cher

Neufchâtel

Fourme de Montbrison

Beaufort

Brocciu / *fresh cheese*

Brie de Meaux / *soft cheese with a bloomy rind*

Morbier / *uncooked pressed cheese*

Munster / *soft cheese with a washed rind*

Beaufort / *hard cheese*

Fourme de Montbrison / *blue cheese*

Pont-l'évêque / *soft cheese with a washed rind*

Laguiole / *uncooked pressed cheese*

Roquefort / *blue cheese*

Cheese Families

In the English-speaking world, we categorize cheeses according to their firmness; in France, cheeses are distinguished according to their manufacturing method.

FRESH CHEESES

Rindless cheeses that are not pressed, cooked, or ripened to maintain their fresh creamy texture:
- Curd cheese, fromage frais, fromage blanc, faisselle, fresh tomme, cottage cheese;
- Pulled curd cheeses (especially Italian cheeses).

SOFT-RIND CHEESES

During manufacture, these cheeses are neither cooked nor pressed. The fresh cheese is allowed to mature, creating an interior with a supple texture. These cheeses include:
- Cheeses with creamy interiors and bloomy rinds (rinds with a soft white downy rind): Camembert, Brie, Coulommiers, Chaource, etc;
- Cheeses with creamy interiors and washed rinds (which are soft, thick, and colorful): Pont l'Évêque, Époisses, Livarot, Maroilles, Trou du Cru, etc;
- Cheeses with creamy interiors and natural rinds (especially goat's milk cheeses): Chabichou, Crottin de Chavignol, Selles-sur-Cher, Pélardon, etc.

PRESSED CHEESES

These cheeses are pressed several times to remove the whey to achieve a dense, rich interior:
- Uncooked pressed cheeses: the milk is heated to under 104°F, then the curds are pressed and matured: Cantal, Morbier, Ossau Iraty, Reblochon, etc;
- Semi-cooked pressed cheeses: the milk is heated to no more than 122°F, then the curds are pressed and matured: Abondance, Cheddar, Leerdammer, Appenzeller, Tête de Moine, etc;
- Cooked pressed cheeses (the curds and whey are heated to over 122°F, then pressed, salted, and matured): French Emmental, Comté, Beaufort, Swiss Gruyère, Portuguese Évora, among others.

BLUE CHEESES

During production, the curds are sprinkled with bacteria and pierced to help the Penicillium bacteria to develop. This creates the blue veins within cheeses such as Roquefort, Gorgonzola, and Stilton, among others.

Following spread:
Barousse cheeses made by Louis Record in Sost in the Pyrenees (Department 65).

Other Cheese Classifications

In France, raw milk cheeses are also differentiated from pasteurized milk cheeses, and fermier (or farmstead) cheeses from dairy cheeses (see page 57). The cheese trade magazine in France, *Profession Fromager*, proposed a classification based on the different levels of coagulation achieved during the production process, from the moment the cheese is drained to the various techniques used to manufacture and ripen it.

In the course of cheese manufacture, milk is first left to acidify, then an enzyme, rennet, is added to break down the milk protein, casein. This disturbs the structure of milk, destabilizing its suspended particles, or micelles, which are composed of an assortment of molecules. This leads to coagulation and the creation of an agglomerate, which, in turn, leads to the formation of curds, a form of gel that contains the protein, fats, lactose, and minerals required to make cheese.

CURD CHEESES

These cheeses are produced by the slow, spontaneous coagulation of the milk:
- Rindless curd cheeses (Rove des Garrigues, Saint-Florentin, Fontainebleau, Boursin, Tartare, etc);
- Bloomy rind cheeses (Chaource, Neufchâtel, Sainte-Maure de Touraine, Selles-sur-Cher, Pouligny-Saint-Pierre, Saint-Félicien, etc);
- Washed or natural rinds (Époisses, Soumaintrain, Langres, Picodon).

RENNET CHEESES

The coagulation of these cheeses is accelerated using rennet. Here we may distinguish:
- Soft cheeses without rinds (Feta, Crescenza); bloomy rind cheeses (Camembert, Brie, Coulommiers); washed, smeared, salted, or natural rinds (Munster, Maroilles, Livarot, Mont d'Or, Pont l'Évêque);
- Uncooked pressed cheeses with a supple interior (Reblochon, Saint-Nectaire, Morbier, Saint-Paulin, Tomme de Savoie, etc.); cheeses with a firm interior (Gouda, Fontina, Raclette, Tomme de Chèvre); or cheeses with a broken curd (Cantal, Salers, Cheddar, Laguiole);
- Semicooked pressed cheeses (Abondance, Appenzeller);
- Cooked pressed cheeses (Comté, Beaufort, Pecorino, Emmental);
- Blue cheeses (Fourme, Roquefort, Persillé des Aravis, Stilton, Gorgonzola, etc).

Facing page: Cutting cow's milk curds in a copper cauldron at Nathalie Espoune's cheese workshop in Ferrières in the Pyrenees (Department 65).

—◆◆—

THE VITAL INGREDIENT: MILK

Milk is a natural secretion from female mammals' mammary glands after birth, in both animals and humans. The liquid provides newborn children with the nutrition they require. The nature of the milk also changes over time to adapt to the growing baby's changing needs. Without milk, there can be no cheese worth its name. But can you make cheese with milk from all animals? And when you do not like or you cannot digest milk, should you remove cheese entirely from your diet?

No Cheese without Milk

Among all mammals, milk is a food rich in calcium, phosphorus, lactose, fats, and proteins. However, it is the K-casein present only in the milk of certain ruminants that enables milk to be transformed into cheese; otherwise it stays liquid.

Casein is the main protein in milk (80 percent) and is responsible for milk's white color. It plays a fundamental role in the transformation of milk into dairy products, such as yogurt and cheese. There are different types of caseins and it is because of Kappa casein, in particular, that proteins organize into micelles in the milk. The destabilization of K-casein micelles during lactic coagulation forms an agglomerate: the curd. Proteins are then broken down into smaller proteins during maturation; this process is called "proteolysis."

Note:
The word milk on its own refers to cow's milk. For other mammals, the name of the species is also used: goat's milk, ewe's milk, etc.

Lactose

Lactose is the main carbohydrate in milk. During digestion, it is broken down using an enzyme—lactase—to form lactic acid. This is what is known as lactic acid fermentation. This lowers the pH and provides the right conditions for different bacteria to develop. Lactose exists in all mammal milk in amounts that vary from one animal to the next, 40 to 45 percent of the dry weight.

Lactose Intolerance

Digestive troubles and "lactose intolerance" caused by milk are due to milk's high lactose content and a deficiency of the lactase enzyme in the gut. Increasing numbers of people are lactose intolerant, so now it is omitted from many product ingredients. Contrary to popular belief, however, you do not have to give up milk and milk products forever if you are lactose intolerant. Small amounts can be tolerated (up to ½ ounce of lactose, i.e. the amount in 1 cup of milk) without problems. Most acute sufferers can replace milk with yogurts and cheeses, as they are made from fermented milk and contain no, or very little, lactose.

Milk's White Color

Composed of 90 percent water, milk is white because of the components in suspension, such as proteins, fats, and sugars, which reflect certain frequencies of light but absorb others. The way the rays of light react varies depending on the components of the milk, which affects the final color. This explains why full-cream, semi-skim, or skim milks have slightly different colors. Skim milk has a slightly bluish color because it contains fewer fats and its calcium-rich protein, casein, is smaller, which means it reflects low-frequency light waves, i.e. the color blue. To conclude: the fewer the fats, the less white milk is.

Milk color is also related to the species of animal and what it eats. The milk of corn-raised cows will be less ivory in color than that of cows grazing in pastures, because grass is high in carotene, a natural pigment of milk.

Why Goat's Cheese is Whiter than Cow's Milk Cheese

Goat's milk and goat's cheese are so white because goats do not assimilate the carotene in grass in the same way as cows: the carotene passes into cow's milk but not goat's milk. Furthermore, goat's cheese is often matured for shorter periods so its interior does not have the time to evolve, hence the white texture.

Whey

Facing page (above left): The lane to the Saraillé organic goat farm in Durban, Gascony, run by the Schihin family; *(above right):* Milk with rennet added before it separates into curds and whey; *(bottom left):* Weaned kid goats at supper time; *(bottom right):* One of the Schihins' goats greeting the camera.

Whey is the clear liquid that forms on the surface of yogurts. During the cheese-making process, it is the liquid part of the milk that remains after coagulation. Full-cream milk contains everything necessary to help young mammals grow. When it is curdled to make cheese, all its components (proteins, vitamins, carbohydrates, minerals, and calcium) divide between the curds and the whey. As a result, the whey contains ten times less fat and four times less protein than milk. It is however high in lactose, rich in potassium, low in sodium, and still contains some of the vitamins of milk. During digestion, the lactose in the whey is transformed into lactic acid, which is an excellent laxative and also helps the body absorb calcium and magnesium. The low fat content of whey makes it a low-calorie food and makes for an excellent detox fix for the body.

❖ *The consumption of fresh or powdered whey helps maintain fitness. Some even use whey as a skin cleanser, while whey-rich baths can help soothe skin irritations, eczema, and rashes.*

Cheesemaking Properties of some Milk

Only some ruminants produce milk that can be transformed into cheese. Such is the case with cows, goats, ewes, and buffaloes, because their milk contains K-casein, which coagulates due to the added rennet to produce curds (see page 26). Although cheese can be made with all milk from cows, goats, buffaloes, or ewes, it is an acknowledged fact that cheese made with different milk from different livestock in different feeding conditions will give a different quality of cheese. There are several determining factors, especially the levels of proteins and butter-fat. The farmer's role is essential here. Farmers know their livestock, their natural cycles, and the influence that seasons and climate can have. An animal's lactation cycle affects the composition of milk. The milk in early lactation is less concentrated than in late lactation. This cycle also depends on what the animal eats.

❖ *Milk from the late lactation phase is higher in fats and will produce a better cheese.*

When Animals Produce Milk

Female cows can only produce milk when they have given birth; their milk is intended to feed their young. A female that does not give birth will not produce milk. This milk production period is called the lactation period. There are "lactation peaks" after calving when milk production is at its highest. Production then gradually decreases to the dry period. The dry period is a time of rest during which the animal stops producing milk; as with human lactation, the dry period arrives when the young have gradually been weaned off their mother's milk and the mother gradually produces less milk before stopping completely. Among milk-producing animals, lactation is a natural cycle that has to be observed and obeyed by farmers to make sure young animals are weaned off their mothers' milk at the right time. The lactation period varies according to the species, their reproduction, and gestation periods.

Facing page:
Dominique Bouchait milking a cow. A Meilleur Ouvrier de France has to have expertise in all areas of the production process.

COWS

Cows are sexually active throughout the year, so there is no precise lactation season. Cows gestate for nine months and produce milk for roughly ten months.

EWES

A ewe's gestation period is five months and their lactation period is six months (from January to June). Ewes have to be dry for at least two months before giving birth, so that the mother's teat can re-form. For cheesemaking, this means that milk is obtained from December to June or July during the transhumance.

GOATS

The gestation period for goats is five months and their lactation period is eight to nine months (from February to September or October). Their lactation peak lasts roughly forty-five days, which explains why cheesemongers' stands are generally brimming with goat cheeses in spring. However, to be able to produce milk year-round, some producers will offset the herd's cycle, either using light or by bringing them into heat.

BUFFALOES

A buffalo's gestation period is eleven months, and the female breastfeeds her young for five months.

The Amount of Milk Needed to Make Cheese

The quantity of milk varies depending on the type of cheese, but also on the animal—cow, goat, ewe, or buffalo—as well as its breed, its grazing conditions on mountains or plains, and the seasons.

CHEESE FROM COWS

About 2½ gallons of milk are needed to create 2¼ pounds of cheese. An average milk cow produces roughly 5¼ gallons of milk per day. High-yield cattle can produce up to 16 gallons of milk per day, but their life expectancy is shorter (five to eight years maximum), whereas regular cows can live ten to fifteen years. High-yield cows also suffer regular complications, such as mastitis.

A single cow can produce 2,100 gallons of milk a year. When milk is purchased to make cheese, it is the weight of the solid matter, rather than the volume, that becomes the reference; after all it is the solid matter that creates the curds.

Facing page: The peak of Mount Spandelles, in the Pyrenees (Department 65), a region producing farmstead mountain cheeses.

Old Wives' Tales
Apparently cows not only produce milk they can also predict the weather: some say that when cows lie down, rain is due.

CHEESE FROM GOATS

There are 1¾ gallons of goat's milk required for 2¼ pounds of cheese. A goat in lactation is milked twice a day and produces between ½ to ¾ gallon of milk a day, so 185 gallons a year. Goats produce double the amount of milk in the spring as they do in the fall.

CHEESE FROM EWES

A ewe is milked twice a day, morning and evening, and, depending on the breed, can produce between ¼ to ¾ gallon of milk a day. To create 2¼ pounds of cheese, you need roughly 1⅓ to 1½ gallons; a single ewe produces between 50 to 80 gallons of milk per year.

CHEESE FROM BUFFALOES

Buffaloes only produce 1½ gallons of milk per day, compared to approximately 5¼ gallons for the average cow! In its biological composition, milk from buffaloes is similar to ewe's milk. With twice the fat content of cow's milk it is harder to work with, but easier to digest, so recommended for low-cholesterol diets (it contains 43 percent less cholesterol than cow's milk). It also has the highest iron, calcium, magnesium, and phosphorus contents of all cheeses. It is possible to make 60 pounds of mozzarella with 26 gallons of buffalo milk, i.e. 2¼ pounds of cheese with 1 gallon of milk.

Did you know?
While buffaloes belong to the bovid family, the buffalo is not a cow and the two species cannot be crossbred. The buffalo is a highly affectionate animal but very stubborn. It loves water and regularly takes mud baths. India and Pakistan are responsible for 90 percent of buffalo milk production in the world.

Facing page:
The author helping out the cheese producer Nathalie Espoune at her farm in the Hautes-Pyrenees. A chance to pick up some great cheeses for market.

Animal Feed and Cheese

Raising cows, goats, ewes, or buffaloes requires special skills. The farmer has to be in a position to respond to their specific needs in varying conditions, as well as to maintain their health. Livestock receive similar treatment to high-level athletes: their diet is controlled and readjusted when necessary. The forage used has to be high quality and as nutritious as possible to stimulate milk production so as to ensure high-quality milk.

Feeding is number one on the list of priorities for cattle breeders, because they need to comply with standards. A well-fed, well-cared-for, healthy animal produces good milk, leading to quality dairy products.

Food Stress

Farmers also have to be careful about food stress, caused by a sudden change of diet. This can give rise to gastric issues, which affect milk quality. During the winter, ewes eat straw and cereals inside, so when they are put out to pasture in the spring, the sudden change of diet may upset their digestion; hence the first cheeses of spring are sometimes of lower quality.

❖ *The food that farmers give their herds can have an impact on the taste of the milk and, therefore, of the cheeses. The botanical diversity of a herd's diet also has a great influence on milk, altering the taste and texture of cheeses. Hence cheese production is a sum of many elements: the soil and climate, the breed of animal and their food, and human labor and know-how.*

In Figures

The cow is a ruminant that grazes eight hours a day and ruminates at rest between nine and twelve hours a day. A milk cow weighing 880 pounds will drink between 20 to 25 gallons of water a day and eat 130 to 175 pounds of food for which the cow produces 50 gallons of saliva to digest.

WHAT A MILK COW EATS

In the fine season, a cow's main food is composed of green forage (grass, alfalfa, and rapeseed). In summer, the herds live outside, either in the alpine pasture (during the transhumance) or in the prairies where they eat wild grasses. Depending on the local climate and the nature of the soil, the pasture period may stretch from four to nine months.

Facing page:
Cows eating hay on their return from the prairie. The farmer will take advantage of this moment to milk them.

In winter, or during a drought-stricken summer, pasture grazing is replaced with hay. Hay production—scything down grass, drying it in the sun, harvesting it, and conservation—also requires the farmer's expertise. In winter, herds are fed inside. They eat:

• silage: forage, which is ground down and stored in silos where it is preserved with acidification with zero oxygen (this type of feed is seldom recommended);

• grasses and legumes (dried forage wrapped in plastic to protect it from the air).

The remainder of their diet is about 25 percent corn silage, as well as energy-rich cereal grains. Minerals and vitamins may also be added to the forage or provided to cows as "mineral licks"—rocks of salts and minerals strategically placed for cows to lick during the day. The one thing all these approaches have in common is to ensure that the animal consumes varying degrees of nutrients, depending on their needs. All these approaches enable high-quality milk production while optimizing yield. Bone meal and antibiotic additives are strictly prohibited.

WHAT A GOAT EATS

Goats have very specific needs and farmers have come to understand how essential their diet is to milk quality. Their daily diet is often "made to measure." Goats are well cared for every day; otherwise, high-quality milk would not be possible. Like cows, goats are also ruminants with an insatiable appetite. A 130-pound milk-producing goat has a small appetite, however. A daily ration of 5¾ pounds dry foodstuffs—hay, alfalfa, dehydrated alfalfa, corn, and barley—is enough. The proportions depend on four main criteria that are revised every day:

• the physical state of each goat;

• the quantity of feed each needs;

• the quantity of milk produced by each goat and its quality;

• the consistency of the goat's feces and the herd's behavior.

In figures

Over the course of ten days, a goat will produce its own weight in milk—proportionally twice as much as a cow. However, goats can only produce milk 240 days a year, from March to October.

Facing page:
An organic goat farm, where natural rearing conditions are respected. Note that the female goats have horns.

WHAT A EWE EATS

Ewes are also ruminants and, like goats, when producing milk, require a diet rigorously adapted to suit their needs, before, during, and after gestation. A ewe needs about 4½ pounds of food a day. A typical ration is composed of hay, legumes, and silage. Farmers use the best forage and take care to gradually phase in foods with a higher nitrogen content to stimulate lactation and achieve higher quality milk.

WHAT A BUFFALO EATS

A buffalo eats 33 to 35 pounds of nitrogen-rich dry matter a day, with 20 percent fiber. For energy, there are cereals and corn. During the summer, the buffaloes go out to pasture, which produces more protein-rich milk.

Thanks to its morphology and hooves, the buffalo is suited to softer terrain and can even graze in swampland. A buffalo will only offer her (abundant) milk if her young is beside her. During gestation and lactation, a buffalo's milk is regularly evaluated and her food is adjusted in the event of an imbalance. Generally, ratios of 3 ounces per 34 ounces of milk for fat content and 1½ ounces per 34 ounces of milk of protein content.

Livestock Breed and Cheese Quality

Some breeds of livestock do stand out when it comes to cheese quality.

COWS

Comté, Abondance, Bleu de Gex, and Reblochon cheese are all the work of the **Montbeliard** breed of cow. The Montbeliard is a fertile breed with a long life expectancy and is very resistant to diseases such as mastitis. The breed frequently appears in the AOP cheese list.

The **Latarin**, or **Tarine**, is a mountain breed that gives a very high-fat milk, enabling the production of the flavorful Beaufort. It is the only breed whose milk contains rare variations of casein, producing a thick, yellow, aromatic, and more intense and animal milk with a variety of aromas.

The **Abondance** also produces a milk that is rich in fats and proteins at levels ideal for a good cheese yield.

In the north, the **Rouge Flamande** and the **Bleue du Nord** both produce protein-rich milk used in the production of northern specialties like Maroilles, Bergues, and Mimolette.

Two identical cheeses created with milk from two different breeds of cow will have different flavors. Let us compare, for example, two Pont l'Évêques, one produced with milk from a Normande cow and the other from a Prim'Holstein:

Facing page: Cows in their stable. Some are more curious about photographers than others.

• The Normande cow has a lower milk yield but the interior of its cheese is dense with a melting texture and an intense odor, while the cheese is highly flavorful with complex aromas.

• The Prim'Holstein has a high milk yield but the interior of its cheese is elastic and sticky with a strong flavor of yeast, without aromatic complexity or pronounced flavor.

The ratio of fat to dry matter and of proteins to butterfat is better in the Normande cow.

❖ *A cow yielding milk with a high casein content offers excellent prospects for cheesemaking. While other cows may produce higher yields of cheese, the product will probably not be as flavorful. Cheese made with protein-rich milk will have the best taste.*

EWES

Like cows, the different breeds produce very different milk. The Lacaune ewe produces tangy blue Roquefort and is the breed with the highest milk yield.

In the southwestern Pyrenees, there are three main milk-producing breeds—the **Basco-béarnaise**, **Black-Faced Manech**, and the **Red-Faced Manech**—which produce Ossau Iraty cheese. The Basco-béarnaise is highly suited to transhu-

Above: A shack where shepherds take shelter and rest close to their flocks during the summer months.

mance, and spends each summer in the high pastures of the Béarn region. The Black-Faced Manech spends more time in the mountains and occupies the harder-to-reach territories of the Basque mountains. The Red-Faced Manech, which lives on the Basque slopes where grass is abundant, has the most abundant milk production of the three. Highly adapted to their habitat, these three breeds produce different quantities of milk with very different nutritional profiles.

GOATS

Once upon a time, goat breeds were very much region-bound: there was the Cévennes white, or the Cou-clair du Berry, the Poitevine, the Massif Central breed, the Catalan goat, and the Pyrenees goat which was also occasionally bred for meat. Depending on climates and the grazing quality of their territories, the quality of their milk varies from one breed to another. The milk of the Rove goat from the Bouches-du-Rhône region is a rustic breed that produces a low milk yield, but it is much sought after for its quality and nutritional content. Its milk is used to produce regional goat's cheeses such as Pélardon, Picodon, and Banon. Two very common breeds of goat in France are the alpine chamois and the Saanen. Both adapt perfectly to stabling and pasture. They produce milk in quantity and quality, and adapt well to more intensive breeding—the farmer's dream! The Saanen produces cheese with a light caprine flavor like the Chabichou, Chavignol, and Pouligny Saint Pierre. The Alpine Chamois gives more solid cheeses.

Transhumance and the Quality of Milk and Cheese

The transhumance is the herds' seasonal change of pasture, when they set off to new grazing lands outside for the summer and the early fall (June through October). The animals feed on a variety of fresh grasses and produce aromatic creamy milk. Furthermore, living in the open air encourages greater physical activity than in the winter, which affects the quality and flavor of the milk and makes it especially protein-rich. Cheese made with milk from the transhumance period has an intense flavor with a variety of notes on the palate. This is why the beginning of the transhumance, when the animals set out for richer pastures, is celebrated with its own special festivities in many French villages. In Beaufortain, for example, cows parade through the village adorned with bells and garlands of flowers.

———— ◆◆ ————

RAW OR PASTEURIZED MILK: WHAT DIFFERENCE DOES IT MAKE TO CHEESE?

Raw, pasteurized, thermized, sterilized, or UHT: Milk can be processed in several ways for preservation or for the creation of dairy products. What transformations does the milk undergo? When does milk need processing? Why are different methods applied? And how do we choose which makes the best cheese?

Raw Milk Cheese

Raw milk does not undergo transformation. It is as pure as the milk from the udder, so is never heated above 104°F. Due to its natural bacteria, cheese develops a variety of aromas and unique textures. Most farmstead, or *fermier*, cheeses are raw milk, the use of which is specified in AOP regulations.

> *Did you know?*
> **Raw milk is a very fragile liquid and has to be used within twelve hours of milking. If refrigerated immediately at 39°F it can be preserved for twenty-four hours.**

Once upon a time, .03 ounce of raw milk contained one million germs. Today, raw milk only contains 15,000—150,000 thousand, due to machine milking, which is more hygienic than manual milking: the milk has limited contact with the air and the storage materials are sterilized and sealed. For cheesemakers, the germs in milk are both a blessing and a bane. A raw milk cheese is not always a happy cheese. In the right hands, raw milk produces magnificent cheeses, as long as cheesemakers are rigorous in their methodology.

Pasteurizing Milk

Used for a variety of foods, pasteurization is a process that destroys a certain number of microorganisms (bacterial flora) naturally present in foods. Milk is pasteurized by heating it to high temperatures for a specified time then rapidly cooling it (162°F for 15 seconds). The process is tested to verify that a natural enzyme, alkaline phosphatase, is now inactive.

> *Did you know?*
> **Louis Pasteur accidentally came across his eponymous conservation process, "pasteurization," while working on a way to stabilize wines. Napoleon III had entrusted him with a mission to cure the "wine diseases" that were posing problems for French winegrowers. He proved that heating wine reduced the levels of contaminants. The technique helped improve wine preservation and was patented by Pasteur in 1871. Pasteur, however, did not think to adapt it to milk, and it was only fifteen years later that the German chemist Franz von Soxhlet encouraged him to heat milk to limit the transmission of pathogens.**

Pasteurized and Sterilized Milk

Sterilized milk is heated to higher temperatures (284 to 302°F) than pasteurized milk by steaming for one second before instant chilling. The process is used for the long-term preservation of milk in bottles, creating Ultra High Temperature (UHT) milk. It is never used in cheesemaking. Milk-processing techniques have diversified over time in order to improve preservation.

Thermization

Thermization is a method of sanitizing raw milk with low heat to create a milk somewhere between raw milk and pasteurized milk. The milk is heated to 140°F for 15 seconds (and not to 113°F for 30 minutes or 162°F for a second, as in pasteurization). The aim is to destroy only a part of the bacteria, such as pathogens like listeria, to make the product safe.

Like pasteurization, thermization modifies the character of milk and its diversity, but leaves more of its technical characteristics: thermized milk generally gives a better-quality product that is more flavorful than pasteurized milk.

Pasteurized Milk Cheeses Compared to Raw Milk Cheeses

Milk pasteurization has the advantage of eliminating bad bacteria, but it also eliminates good bacteria responsible for the development of fine flavors and aromas. When lactose is broken down during the ripening process, or *affinage*, each bacterium produces a different aroma. This explains why raw milk cheeses do not have the same flavor as those made from pasteurized milk: without bacteria in the milk, pasteurized milk cheeses cannot develop the same wide range of aromas and flavors as raw milk cheeses.

By using pasteurized milk, the producer knows the cheese will be less flavorful than raw or thermized milk, but it won't necessarily be a bad cheese. There are some very good cheeses made with pasteurized milk—just as there are very bad cheeses made with raw milk. Raw milk cheese is not a guarantee of quality and flavor. While from a technical point of view, pasteurized milk has a more limited diversity of options for development than raw milk, a cheese is not just made of milk. Cheesemakers know how to get the best out of their land and herds using their *affinage* skills. By bringing their experience and know-how to the fore, pasteurized milk can produce wonderful cheeses.

> *Did you know?*
> **What milk-producing animals eat is as important as the type of milk used to create cheese: animals that live outside and eat fresh grass and wild plants will produce much more interesting milk than animals raised inside.**

❖ *The diversity in the texture, taste, and aroma of a cheese cannot be reduced to the use of raw or pasteurized milk: they depend on what animals eat, but also what the cheesemaker brings to the cheese during* affinage.

Milk Powder and Cheese

Facing page: Cheese labels note whether the milk is raw, pasteurized, or thermized. This does not apply to AOP cheeses and cooked pressed cheeses. A Comté, for example, is always made with raw milk.

While technically possible, the experiments carried out have not produced anything of quality. Powdered milk is often used to make yogurts; they help to obtain a more solid consistency. Milk is dehydrated into its powdered form to prolong preservation while maintaining its nutritional qualities. It also decreases transport and storage costs and does not require refrigeration.

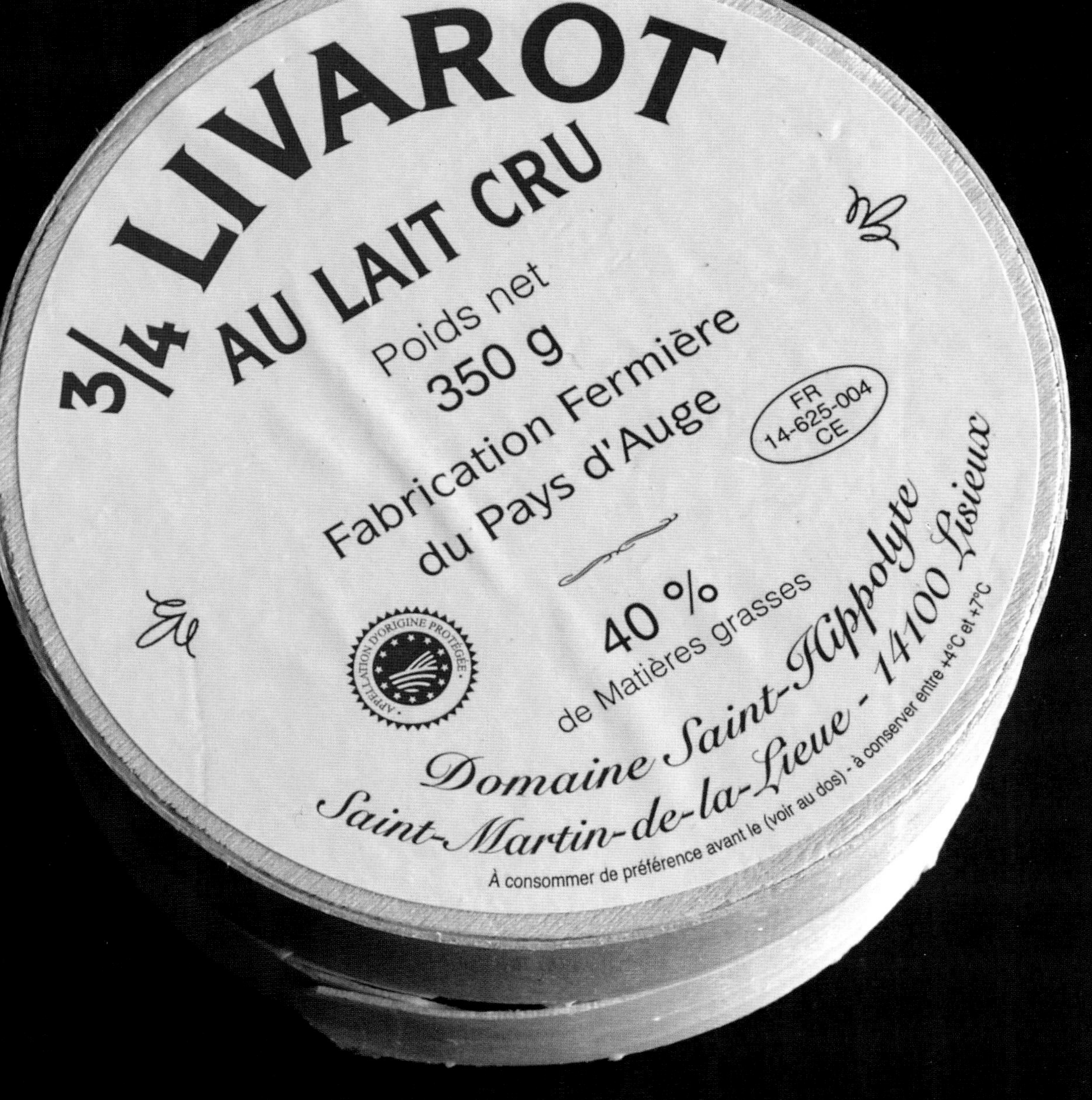

3/4 LIVAROT
AU LAIT CRU
Poids net
350 g
Fabrication Fermière
du Pays d'Auge
FR
14-625-004
CE
40 %
de Matières grasses
APPELLATION D'ORIGINE PROTÉGÉE
Domaine Saint-Hippolyte
Saint-Martin-de-la-Lieue - 14100 Lisieux
À consommer de préférence avant le (voir au dos) - à conserver entre +4°C et +7°C

THE CHEESEMAKING PROCESS

The French expression "to make a whole cheese" is one instance where their gastronomic traditions color their language. The expression translates as "to make a mountain of a molehill," which is effectively what cheesemaking involves. You start with something simple, like milk, and you turn it into something complex: cheese! Whether raw milk, pasteurized, *fermier*, crafted, or dairy, hard or soft, cheese follows a very precise manufacturing process, requiring command and know-how. To vary the pleasures of the palate, cheese also comes in different shapes, sizes, and colors: big and small, round and square, gray, orange, yellow, and white. How come milk turns out so different?

How to Make Cheese

The only production stage shared by all cheeses is curdling. During this stage, milk coagulates when the solids separate from the liquid. Coagulated milk is known as "curds." From this point on, the various processes develop the curds in different ways. These processes are: the addition of rennet, molding, draining, salting, pressing, the addition of lactic acid bacteria, and *affinage*, or ripening.

ADDING RENNET
The use of rennet enables milk to coagulate more quickly. Depending on the quantity and type of rennet used, different structures and textures of curds are achieved. Rennet is traditionally a digestive enzyme extracted from calves' intestines, but it can also be of plant origin, found in thistles, lemons, or figs, or microbial, from mold, enzymes, or bacteria. The addition of rennet is called "renneting."

MOLDING

Molding is essential for soft-rind or hard cheeses. With soft-rind cheeses, the curds are ladled delicately inside the mold; for larger cheeses the molds may be lined with muslin to help to drain the whey. To assist draining, cheeses are also pressed and turned.

DRAINING

The draining process enables the cheesemaker to control the moistness and thus the firmness and texture of the cheese. Soft and curd cheeses undergo less drainage. It is at this point in the process that the whey (see page 28) is separated from the curd. The whey is then fed back to the young animal as it contains many nutrients essential for the animal's health.

SALTING

While helping to preserve cheeses, salt has other roles to play in cheesemaking:
- It helps draw out the whey in cheese and thus helps draining.
- Applied to the surface of the ripening cheese it helps form the rind, and is added for different lengths of time and at different moments of ripening, depending on the cheese.
- It enables the development of specific floras that help balance flavors and aromas, while also enhancing the taste.

> *Note:*
> **Whether coarse sea salt or table salt, the salt used has to be non-iodized, because iodine prevents the development of the bacteria and yeasts required for fermentation and slows down the process of maturation.**

Salting is carried out in three ways:
- When the cheese is dry, the salt is sprinkled or scattered over the cheese depending on its size;
- By immersion in brine for several hours to several days; saturation in brine is especially used for bigger cheeses;
- It is added to the curds (especially in Salers and Cheddar).

The salt accumulates at the surface of the cheese before migrating toward the middle. In large cheeses this balance is never achieved, making the exterior more flavorful, which is why some clients actively favor rind cuts.

THE ADDITION OF LACTIC ACID BACTERIA

Raw milk has always contained the bacteria necessary for curdling. Constant advances in hygiene have fortunately eliminated most of the harmful bacteria responsible for food-borne illnesses, but this means that today, unlike in the past, that raw milk does not have the same bacteria content for natural curdling. A good bacterial balance is essential for creating quality cheese. Because good bacteria have a vital role to play in curdling, today lactic acid bacteria are added to milk to make it more "cheese-worthy."

These bacteria have an effect, above all, on the flavor, preservation, and quality of the milk. The quantity of ferments is proportional to the number of bacteria eliminated. When milk is pasteurized, the pasteurization process removes a great many bacteria, so more ferments are added to raw milk. Raw milk with all the right bacteria, and requiring no additional ferments, still exists.

AFFINAGE

The aging, maturing, or ripening process is often referred to by its French name, *affinage*. Affinage is an essential stage in the cheesemaking process (see pages 66-67) and has an important technical dimension. The aim is to enhance the flavor of cheese by maturing it in the optimum conditions. Affinage depends on several factors: atmosphere, temperature, and the humidity in caves d'affinage, as well as any treatment the cheesemaker may provide. Soft rinds and bloomy rinds are matured in caves d'affinage with high-humidity (95 percent), whereas washed rinds prefer slightly lower humidity (85 to 90 percent). The ripening duration depends on the type of cheese: soft rinds require an average of two to four weeks; for hard rinds, the process is longer, lasting four months at least, the time it takes for the rind to harden and develop all its aromas.

❖ ***Ripening controls the texture of cheese; those aged for longer periods will be drier.***

Facing page: Milk solidifying. The addition of rennet acidifies the milk, separating the curds from the whey.

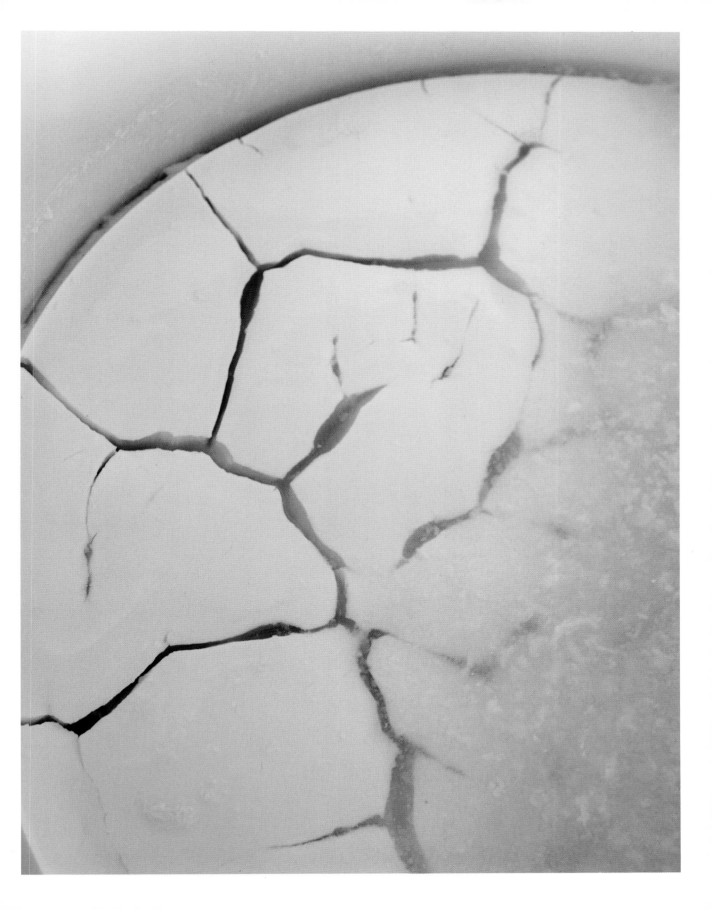

Lactic Acid Bacteria

Lactic acid bacteria include all kinds of useful microorganisms such as bacteria, molds, and yeasts.

BACTERIA

+ **Lactic acid bacteria** are naturally present in raw milk and are the first to develop in cheesemaking. These bacteria acidify milk and help it curdle. They also contribute to the development of the flavor and texture of milk products. They are mainly deployed as a starter culture of selected bacteria added to pasteurized milk or milk lacking the microorganisms necessary.

+ **Propionic acid bacteria** contribute to flavor formation and to the unique development of cooked pressed cheese.

+ Non-pathogenic **micrococci** and **staphylococci** are present on the surface of cheeses. These bacteria have an essential role to play in affinage, especially with washed, bloomy, and mixed- rind cheeses.

YEASTS

Yeasts are much more present outside on the surface of a cheese (especially with soft rind cheeses) than inside and they help the flavor develop.

MOLDS

Mold, the fungal growth rather than the process of shaping the cheese earlier in production, is crucial for the transformation of cheese during *affinage*. Here are the most common molds:

+ *Penicillium camemberti* is sprayed onto the surface of soft and bloomy rind cheeses.

+ *Penicillium roqueforti* is the mold that forms inside blue cheeses and Roquefort.

+ *Mucor* is the dominant mold on the surface of Tomme de Savoie and is also present on the surface of farmstead Saint-Nectaire.

The mold changes the cheese and helps develop its texture and rich flavors. This is the alchemy of the aging process and depends on a series of appraisals and technical interventions on the part of the cheesemaker. Some molds are good for one cheese and bad for another. *Mucor*, for example, is great for Tomme de Savoie, but bad for Camembert.

Facing page (above left): Different types of molds for forming cheese to bring out different flavors; *(above right):* Aging ewe's cheeses. These cheeses are ten days old. Already the rind is beginning to color; *(below left):* Needles are inserted into the cheese to help drain the whey; *(below right):* Muslin bag for molding cheese. The numbers imprinted into the cheese indicate the week the cheese was made.

Did you know?

Today, using biotechnology, aromas can be incorporated into cheese without using mold. So it is possible to make products flavored with blue cheese without the use of *Penicillium roqueforti*. Naturally, to my mind, such blue cheeses do not match up to the real deal.

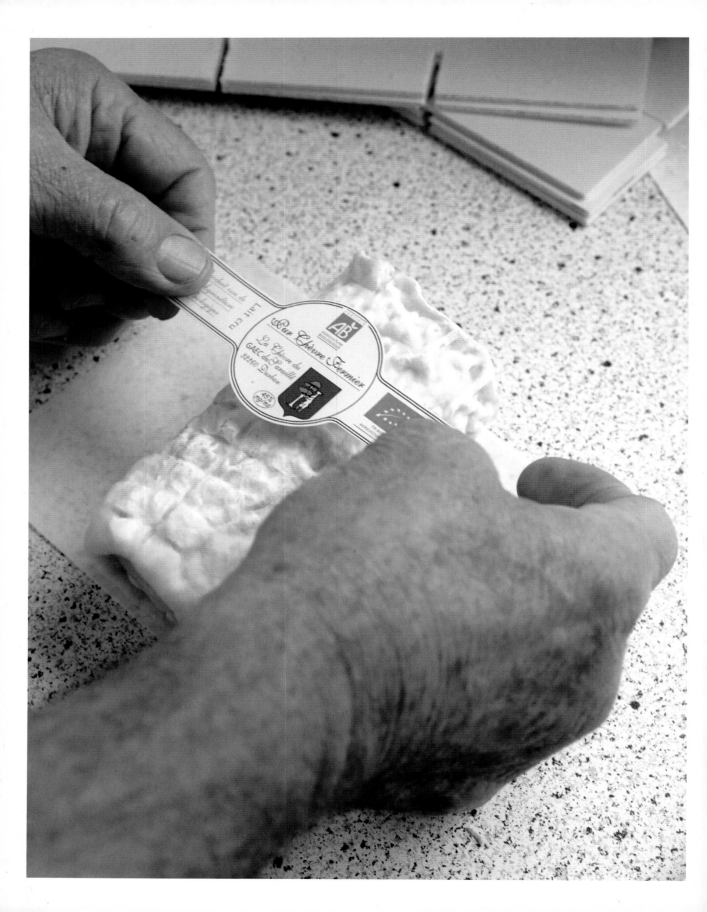

The Difference between Fermier, Artisanal, and Dairy Cheeses

The difference between the three types mainly emerges in their flavor. *Fermier*, or farmstead, cheeses will always be the most flavorful of the three.

FERMIER CHEESE

Also known as farmstead, farmhouse, or *alpage* cheese, these cheeses are produced on the same farm as the herds that produce their milk, and by the farmers who rear the cattle and live there. *Fermier* cheese is made exclusively from a single herd or flock on the farm, so comes from a delimited area and is produced using the family's own, sometimes ancestral, techniques based on what they know of their *terroir*—their land and climate. They know what breeds best suit their terrain. They know the best and most varied diet for them—pasturing during the summer and foraging during the winter. They know how to care for them and their well-being, how best to make cheese from the milk they yield, and how to ripen their product. All these elements help make cheese with great character, which is the hallmark of farmstead cheeses.

ARTISANAL CHEESE

Artisanal cheese refers to cheeses created from milk batches from several herds or flocks raised in close geographic proximity.

DAIRY CHEESE

Dairy cheese (*laitier* in French) is made in a dairy from a mixture of milks purchased from different farms, which can sometimes come from different, distant regions.

❖ **It is often believed that fermier cheese is always better than dairy cheese. Fermier *is not an absolute guarantee of quality however.* Fermier *cheese also varies in quality according to the seasons. A good dairy cheese is always better than a bad farmstead cheese.***

The Variety of Cheeses

Logically humankind first discovered fromage frais or fromage blanc, simple curd cheeses, before they set to work on perfecting their cheese-making techniques. In the process, they will have discovered how to make more solid cheeses suitable for longer storage and conservation (see page 18).

Previous spread: French cheese labels, with storage advice, sell-by-date, provenance, and AOP labeling. *(Left)* An organic raw milk *fermier* goat's cheese. *(Right)* A raw milk AOP *fermier* Munster.

Facing page: The hands of Nathalie Espoune turning a 8¾ pound wheel of cheese. It is a delicate procedure: the cheese has only been pressed for thirty minutes and the texture is still crumbly.

Over time, cheese diversified into many different types. Textures became harder and more complex. Soft-rind cheeses were born, and then came uncooked pressed cheeses and cooked pressed cheeses with varying degrees of firmness. We then developed ripening techniques, which vary according to regions and *terroirs*. In the North, different washes were developed with Normandy cider used for Camembert while Marc de Bourgogne liquor came into use for Epoisses. The aging and molding processes created different sizes and textures of cheese, a reflection of different populations' needs in terms of what they ate and for how long they had to preserve their food.

❖ *Cheeses became more varied for several reasons: occasionally because of chance, but above all because of the development of cheesemaking techniques; then factors such as regional customs, human necessity in the face of a specific climate, geographic location, and lifestyles had an impact.*

Cheese Sizes and Shapes

There is a huge difference between cheeses of the mountains and of the plains. Cheeses made in the mountains are produced by a whole family or even community in which the work is shared (see next page) and the cheese is produced to respond to the community's need for sustenance throughout the winter. Cheeses from the more populated lowlands are produced for regular day-to-day consumption, and so offer a greater variety of shapes and colors.

While some regions, like Normandy, for example, have become loci for the intensive production of small-size cheeses, it is no doubt because this size of cheese suits the needs of their populations, much greater than in mountainous areas. With supply related to demand, it is more logical to create a larger number of smaller cheeses when you have many mouths to feed than to ripen cheeses for long-term storage.

In the mountains, life is very different. The population is less dense and more scattered, leading to lower consumption and a need to store foods for longer. Common sense and necessity have therefore been the mothers of invention in the mountains, where cheeses are made larger, for longer-term storage—sometimes up to a year—to provide for more dispersed and less accessible communities.

❖ *By observing the size and firmness of a cheese you can easily tell if it was made in the high-mountains, mountains, valley countryside, or plains.*

Facing page: A 90-pound Cantal that has been molded in linen. We can see the imprint of the linen on the rind.

The shapes differ from one cheese to the next and one region to the next because farmers used anything available to mold cheese. Methods and tools evolved and the shape of some cheeses changed. While shape helps identify a cheese, it also influences flavor. Truncated cones, *crottins*, pyramids, or logs are all shapes that have been long studied during their ripening processes.

Climate, Seasons, and Cheese Production

Seasons and climates are essential factors in cheese manufacture, with a key role to play in the way aromas develop; cheesemakers develop finely honed skills of observation to read the telltale signs. Climate and vegetation vary according to the region. Every small area of France conceals natural treasures and the nutrition that pastures offer changes with the seasons. Weather is also an important factor: summer storms can indeed "turn" milk.

Each season involves a different diet. Each change in diet affects the composition of the milk and its ability to be transformed.

SPRING

Spring is a time of resurrection and abundance. Even if the grass is not yet high, it is still tender and varied, rich in carbohydrates, and low in cellulose, which leads to dietary supplements in fibers and magnesium, using dry forage to satisfy ruminants' natural needs.

Facing page: A mountain scene. To the north, there are clouds out of shot and more vegetation; to the south the grass is scarce.

Cows, goats, and ewes supply an abundance of rich, fragrant milk. After calving, milk yields are at their peak and traditional and industrial production is at its opti-

mum output. The *caves d'affinage* once more fill with cheeses, and the *affineurs* responsible for maturing them wash and rub soft surfaces and turn the wheels to drain them. Spring cheeses contain more water and are thus creamier than in the fall and in winter.

SUMMER

During the summer, grass is abundant and the pasture flora of wild flowers like gentian, blue thistle, and broom, and aromatic herbs like thyme and rosemary, lend the milk their subtle aromas, so apparent in fresh cheeses like Fontainebleau, Jonchée, and Brousse du Rove, with their delicate flavors. Summer milk is the best: at the end of lactation the animal's milk is full of butterfat and rich in proteins. Farmers have to be sensitive to weather conditions, however. If the weather is too dry, the grasses dry out and lose their nutritional value leading to a decreased milk yield; a rainy summer engorges the grass with water bringing milk in abundance but with a lower content of milk solids, especially proteins; in storm periods, the milk becomes sharper in taste, making cheese rinds tighter and interiors less creamy. Whatever the weather, cheesemakers have to adapt their approach. Along the Mediterranean, for example, producers of the Pélardon goat's cheese fear the humid southern winds. When the wind blows in from the sea over several days, it becomes harder to drain the curds and unwanted bacteria can form. With the mistral, however, "cheese makes itself."

> *Did you know?*
> **Fromage frais never has a rind because it has not been matured. Its water content is thus higher and so it is lower in calories.**

FALL

In the fall, the herds and flocks return to their barns or folds. It is the time when lactation ceases for many animals. The ground is dry and pasture inadequate. To meet ruminants' needs, their grass diet has to be supplemented with dry forage, providing fiber and magnesium as in the spring. Low milk production yields seasonal cheeses such as Vacherin Mont d'Or and Morbier.

WINTER

Winter is a period of transition for many cheeses. Animals return to their barns and folds where they are fed hay and silage. This is the period when their feeding is most monitored to maintain the quality of the milk. A cheese produced in winter

Facing page: The stable at 6 a.m. There is no waiting for the rooster to crow before setting to work.

has a very different flavor and color to a cheese produced in the summer. The carotene in the forage lends it a yellow hue. Some purists will only consume summer milk, but winter milk is still very good—after all, hay is simply dried summer grass, so it is more aromatic and thus more capable of creating delicious cheese.

> *Goat's Cheese and Christmas in France*
> **The goat's cheese season runs from late spring to early fall, a period when it is most flavorful. Unfortunately we live in a consumer society that demands a constant supply of goods throughout all seasons. So, some producers alter the goats' natural lactation cycle with hormone injections and light, or use frozen curds.**

Camemberts around France

Technically it is possible to produce a Camembert-style cheese in the south of France, even though its natural home is Normandy. Australia also produces great Camembert cheeses: the bloomy rind technique exports very well. What differs is the flavor, which is directly related to the *terroir*—the soil, climate, and vegetation—and what the cows eat, the breed of cow, and the regional techniques deployed to adapt to regional conditions. This is why Camembert de Normandie is an AOP, a protected appellation. So, it is possible to copy the Camembert recipe to create similar, and very good, cheeses, but it is impossible to produce a Normandy Camembert with the same organoleptic qualities as the northern variety. What's more, there is very little point in trying.

Facing page: Two Camemberts de Normandie from the same producer, made on the same day. They are, however, very different.

———◆◆———

AFFINAGE AND PRESERVATION

Affinage is a crucial stage in the life of a cheese and preserving cheeses is a problem in the absence of regulated caves d'affinage, with their constant lower temperatures and relative humidity. How are cheeses preserved without altering their flavors while also being protected from environmental odors? How do we know if a cheese has been sufficiently ripened before buying and consuming it? Can the ripening process be continued at home?

The Purpose of Affinage

Maturing cheeses means aging them and ripening them—the French term we shall use here is *affinage*. Ripening helps cheeses to develop their flavor and delicious textures. A cheese is said to be ripe, or *affiné*, when it reaches optimal maturity during the ripening process. This varies among cheeses and depends on the different periods of the year. A Camembert de Normandie that is *affiné à cœur*, or "ripe to the heart," means that the texture of its interior is perfectly and completely soft and smooth: it is ready to be consumed in the perfect conditions.

❖ *Cheeses are aged either at the farm or dairy where they were made, or the affineur takes care of them. The cheesemonger who sells the cheese may also ripen cheeses in their own caves d'affinage or boutique. All the expertise of the professional comes to the fore in this crucial ripening stage, during which the cheese undergoes great transformation due to the love and attention required for perfect ripening.*

Which Cheeses Need Ripening?

All cheeses undergo *affinage*, with the exception of fromages frais or fromages blancs. A fromage frais is literally a "fresh" cheese, one whose curds have just separated from the whey and drained. Ripening a cheese means taking it from this state and aging it to develop a rind, so that the sometimes bland, aromaless curds turn into a flavorful, fragrant, beautifully textured cheese. Each family of cheeses requires different attention.

Why some Cheeses Need Ripening

Ripening helps preserve cheeses for longer periods of time and develops their aromas and flavors. Cheesemakers have to control this evolution. There are two types of ripening procedures.

SURFACE *AFFINAGE*

Of the two methods, this is quickest, but it is less stable. Enzymes are applied to the surface of the cheese, and gradually make their way into the center. This is how *affineurs* create bloomy rinds with their downy Brie-like white coats, or washed rinds, with their smooth, glossy exteriors and beautiful yellow hues.

INTERIOR *AFFINAGE*

This method is slower but more stable. Some cheeses can be matured for months, even years, before being consumed.

Cheese-Ripening Variability

Each cheese requires special ripening. The duration of cheese ripening differs between families of cheeses and products: some are ripened for only a few days (especially small cheeses), while others take much longer.

Ripening time is directly related to the properties of the milk, the breed of the animal, the way its milk was produced, the cheesemaker's techniques, and local attributes such as the weather, the season, and even the condition of the building where the cheese was produced. During maturation, each type of cheese requires different temperatures and relative humidity in the *caves d'affinage*, or ripening rooms. These range from high-tech temperature-controlled chambers to famous cellars, to natural caves in the rock.

Following spread (left): Cheeses in Schihin farm ripening room in Durban (Department 32). A quality rind should not be too moist or too dry; *(right):* Two logs of goat's cheese produced eight days apart at the Schihin farm.

LIST OF *AFFINAGE* TIMES FOR AOP CHEESES

CHEESES	AOC DATE*	MINIMUM *AFFINAGE***	OPTIMUM *AFFINAGE*
Abondance	1990	100 days after renneting	6 months
Banon	2003	15 days after renneting	4 weeks
Beaufort	1968	5 months	6 to 9 months
Bleu d'Auvergne, less than 2¼ pounds	1975	2 weeks	4 weeks
Bleu d'Auvergne, more than 2¼ pounds	1975	4 weeks	8 weeks
Bleu de Gex Haut-Jura, or Bleu de Septmoncel	1977	21 days after molding	2 months
Bleu des Causses	1991	70 days after molding	6 months
Bleu du Vercors-Sassenage	1998	21 days	4 weeks
Brie de Meaux	1980	4 weeks after molding	8 weeks
Brie de Melun	1980	4 weeks after molding	2 months
Brocciu, or Brocciu corse	1983	0	0
Brocciu passu	1983	21 days	6 weeks
Camembert de Normandie	1983	22 days after renneting	4 weeks
Cantal jeune	1956	30 to 60 days	
Cantal entre-deux	1956	90 to 210 days	
Cantal vieux	1956	plus 240 days	
Chabichou du Poitou	1990	10 days after renneting	6 weeks
Chaource	1970	2 weeks to after molding	40 to 60 days
Charolais	2010	16 days after renneting	6 weeks
Chavignol, or Crottin de Chavignol	1976	10 days after molding	4 weeks
Chevrotin	2002	21 days after renneting	4 to 5 weeks
Comté	1958	4 months after renneting	12 months
Époisses	1991	4 weeks after molding	6 to 8 weeks
Fourme d'Ambert	1972	28 days	3 months
Fourme de Montbrison	1972	32 days after renneting	6 weeks
Laguiole	1961	4 months after renneting	6 to 9 months
Langres	1991	15 to 21 days according to the format	When the fountain is ¼ inch deep

* Appelation d'Origine Contrôlé (AOC) was founded in 1935, and is the former French label for food products, guaranteeing their origin. The AOP described earlier is the European version of the AOC. Today all AOC French cheeses have been relabeled AOP.

CHEESES	AOC DATE*	MINIMUM *AFFINAGE***	OPTIMUM *AFFINAGE*
Trois-quarts and *petit Livarot*	1975	*21 days after renneting*	*5 weeks*
Livarot and *grand Livarot*	1975	*35 days after renneting*	*5 weeks*
Mâconnais	2006	*10 days after unmolding*	*3 to 4 weeks*
Maroilles	1976	*5 weeks after molding*	*3 months*
Mont d'Or, or vacherin du Haut-Doubs	1981	*21 days after renneting*	*5 weeks*
Morbier	2000	*45 days after molding*	*9 to 10 weeks*
Petit munster	1969	*14 days after renneting*	*5 weeks*
Munster or munster-géromé	1969	*21 days after renneting*	*7 weeks*
Neufchâtel	1969	*10 days after molding*	*4 to 5 weeks*
Ossau-iratyy, 8¾ to 15½ pounds	1980	*120 days after molding*	*240 days*
Ossau-iraty, 4½ to 6¾ pounds	1980	*80 days after molding*	*160 days*
Pélardon	2000	*11 days after renneting*	*2 weeks*
Picodon	1983	*14 days after renneting*	*4 weeks*
Picodon dieulefit	1983	*1 month after renneting*	*4 weeks*
Pont-l'évêque *petit,* *demi* and pont-l'évêque (3 formats)	1972	*18 days*	*6 weeks*
Pont-l'évêque *grand* (one format)	1972	*21 days*	*6 weeks*
Pouligny-saint-pierre	1972	*10 days*	*4 to 5 weeks*
Reblochon de Savoie	1958	*15 days after molding*	*4 to 5 weeks*
Rigotte de Condrieu	2009	*8 days after unmolding*	*3 weeks*
Rocamadour	1996	*6 days after unmolding*	*15 days*
Roquefort	1925 (AO) 1975 (AOC)	*90 days after molding*	*5 to 12 months*
Saint-nectaire	1955	*28 days*	*7 to 8 weeks*
Sainte-maure-de-touraine	1990	*10 days after renneting*	*4 weeks*
Salers	1961	*3 days after unmolding*	*1 year*
Selles-sur-cher	1975	*10 days after renneting*	*3 weeks*
Tome des Bauges	2002	*5 weeks*	*6 to 8 weeks*
Valençay	1998	*11 days after renneting*	*4 weeks*

** The minimum ripening duration is defined by law (in terms of days, weeks, or months, after renneting or molding, etc.).

Climatic conditions are hugely important and affect the weight loss of the cheese, rind formation, and the development of its surface floras.

❖ *Each type of cheese requires different attention depending on its nature and origins to bring out its organoleptic qualities and its characteristic flavor. AOP cheeses follow very strict rules defining the production location, the techniques used, and the minimum ripening times.*

These are drawn up as a list of regulations specific to each AOP cheese.

The Rind

The rind protects the interior and helps the cheese express its flavors to the maximum. During ripening, rinds are often smeared, washed, or brushed depending on their surfaces and the type of cheese involved. This process helps remove the surface moisture of the young cheese.

Eating the Rind

Some rinds are indeed more appealing than others. What matters is the flavor. It is basically up to you if you want to eat the rind or not.

Natural Rind

A natural rind is a rind that has not undergone spraying, washing, or smearing during the ripening process. This applies especially to natural soft-rind cheeses. Otherwise, rinds form due to the intervention of the cheesemaker or *affineur*, who will spray or wash the cheeses: the bloomy rind of the Camembert de Normandie, for example is achieved by spraying *Penicillium camemberti* on the surface to obtain its familiar soft, downy exterior. Other cheeses are washed with brine, such as Ossau-Iraty and Comté.

Facing page: Cheeses ripening. The *affineur* has to care for the rind, washing and brushing it, leaving each cheese enough space to ripen at the correct rate.

Seasons and Affinage

Affinage is hugely dependant on seasonal changes—even caves d'affinage undergo climatic changes. The affineur has to control the caves d'affinage's own microclimate to keep it as stable as possible, closely controlling humidity and temperature. Today caves d'affinage are controlled by elaborate technology, evaporators, humidifiers, refrigeration, and heating. But some still operate in a traditional way, such as in the Roquefort region where the cheese is ripened in the *fleurines* of the natural rock formations.

Did you know?
Fleurines are the natural fissures and cavities in the rock formations that exist in caves and caves d'affinage dug into the rock in the Causse region in southern France. They have an especially effective thermal and hygrometric role to play.

Verifying the Maturity of Cheeses

In order to control maturity during the ripening process, the affineur has a series of tasks to perform that vary according to the cheese:
- Tasting the cheese and checking its firmness. Observing its color and aspect.
- Assessing and adjusting the ambient humidity.
- In the case of Comté, the affineur uses a small hammer to tap the rind and "ring" the wheels, like a bell. From the tones he hears, he can judge whether the cheeses need further aging or if they are ready to be eaten.

Preceding spread (left): A small caves d'affinage with small-scale cheese production. Each cheese is different; *(right):* Three Comtés, aged for six, eighteen, and thirty months.

Facing page: Napoléon Commingeois (a ewe's milk cheese from southwest France) aged for eighteen months. Cheese mites are responsible for its coarse surface and lunar appearance.

CHEESE MITES
For some cheeses, the affineur may deploy flour mites, also known as cheese mites. These miniscule acarians are tamed by the affineur to give a very precise visual indication of the age of cheeses. Cheese mites feed from cheese rind in high-humidity caves d'affinage. Fortunately their breeding can be controlled by temperature adjustment. The colder the caves d'affinage, the less they like it. What is especially useful with the cheese mite is its ability to pierce and change the cheese rind. Their activity helps the rind to breathe and the cheese to develop, creating a more flavorful and aromatic cheese.

Cheese mites are effectively scattered powderlike over the surface of the cheese by the affineur. They will only settle in and breed at a certain late stage in the cheese's development and, at this point, give the rind a dusty beige color.

Maturity and Quality

A cheese's future quality depends on a number of factors that are independent of the aging process. What a cow eats, for example, influences the texture and flavor of cheeses because milk is composed of natural molecules directly or indirectly produced by what is ingested. The manufacturing process also greatly influences the quality of the final product. Draining is one of the most important and delicate stages (see page 49) and hugely affects cheese quality.

❖ *From the raw product to the finished article, each stage of production influences the quality of cheese. Affinage however remains the essential stage, the finishing school as it were, which develops the full potential of the cheese's texture and flavor.*

> *Tips for achieving a flavorful cheese once you get cheese home:*
> A cheese is ripe before it becomes mature. So all cheese lovers can continue this ripening process at home with a few simple tips:
> • Chaource should be stored at room temperature beneath a glass cheese dome (a stick of cinnamon can also be placed beneath the dome alongside the cheese).
> • Wrap a slice of Roquefort in muslin and suspend it above a plate containing sweet white wine: The Roquefort will become infused with the wine's evaporating aromas.
> • Remove a slab of young Reblochon from its wrapping and place it on a wooden board.
> • Turn a Camembert de Normandie every day so that it keeps its original appearance.

Facing page: Ewe's milk cheeses by Claude Espoune (Department 65). In his caves d'affinage, Claude carefully doses light and human presence so that his cheeses can rest for the time they need.

Refrigerating Cheese

The best way to store cheese is to replicate the original conditions of ripening with a temperature between 50 to 54°F and 90 percent humidity. The older a cheese, the more it supports the cold; the younger it is, the more it has to breathe to develop. Yogurts, fromage frais, goat's cheeses, and small cheeses need static refrigeration to ensure preservation. Voluminous cheeses are better stored using ventilated refrigeration. Each type of refrigeration has its advantages and drawbacks for cheese storage:

- Ventilated refrigeration fans non-humid cold air evenly throughout the refrigerator.
- Static refrigeration lets air circulate freely. Warm air rises and cold air sinks. Static refrigeration is recommended for cheeses sensitive to variations in humidity.

What you have to avoid:

- very low temperatures, which hinder the development of the cheese and kill the flavor and odor, and have a negative impact on color, look, and consistency;
- high temperatures, which stimulate secondary fermentation and deteriorate the quality of the cheese.

Advice
In general, you should serve your cheeses at room temperature, i.e. remove them from the refrigerator an hour before eating. This awakens their aromas and lets them breathe.

Wrapping Cheese for Storage

Facing page: A variety of cheese packages (Epoisses, Mont-d'Or, Pélardon, Pont l'Evêque). Make sure to wrap cheeses in suitable waxed paper or parchment paper, which lets cheeses breathe while preventing the rind from cracking or sweating.

The best way to store cheese is to keep it in a wooden box, which naturally maintains the right level of humidity. Otherwise, leave them in their waxed paper or box in a plastic bag and place them in the refrigerator's crisper drawer (the coldest and most humid part of the refrigerator).

Advice
Avoid confined air and sealed plastic boxes.

—◆◆—

TRADITION, FLAVOR, AND TASTING

"What is the best accompaniment for a good cheese?" When one of my employees, Corine, was asked this question, she simply replied, "Somebody who loves cheese!" Good cheese stands alone, but the vast gastronomic depth and variety of cheese mean that it is often served with simple fare: bread, salad, wine, or other simple dishes. When it comes to flavor, the French have very refined palates, and are also very demanding. Although the market has been flooded with cheeses made from pasteurized milk, true cheese lovers still remain loyal to raw milk and are meticulous in their tasting habits.

Why the French Like Raw Milk Cheese

Raw milk cheese has not undergone thermal treatment, so it still contains the bacterial floras that help to develop aromas during ripening. The French love raw milk cheeses so much because of their flavor. Furthermore, raw milk cheese production is an ancestral tradition, part of the history of our regions. For France, defending and protecting these techniques also means preserving its gastronomic heritage. The AOC is also about consumer protection—protecting consumers' right to a diversity of flavors amid the flood of industrialized, pasteurized products which bring blander flavors and standardization.

French Cheeses VS. Cheeses from other Countries

Good cheese can be found everywhere, whether it is made with raw milk or pasteurized milk. Flavor is, of course, a subjective issue, and to say that France makes the best cheeses would be highly misleading. What we do have is a past and regional traditions anchored in their terroir. France references the unique importance of a landscape's soil and climate, the local conditions that affect sensitive agricultural products such as milk, wine, meat, vegetables, and cheese. France is fortunate that the scope and variety of this *terroir*, between mountains and plains, enables us to enjoy a highly diverse range of cheeses, perhaps the most diverse in the world.

Is Cheese Made Everywhere in France?

This is a difficult question to answer. It is impossible to know all French cheeses. Some appear, others disappear, on a weekly basis, and not all have AOP labeling. The regions of lowest cheese production in France are those along the Atlantic Ocean. Here grass is scarcer and livestock breeding rarer.

When Cheeses are at their Best

Today, thanks to refrigeration, efficient distribution networks, better breeding conditions, and modern production techniques, cheeses are available throughout the year. Our gastronomic heritage can now be savored whatever the season, even cheeses made with raw milk. Some raw milk cheeses are indeed produced year-round, but others have optimal times of year.

Certain cheeses have traditionally been produced throughout the year, especially the cooked cheeses made from cow's milk, like Beaufort, Comté, and Emmental, which are then aged for four to thirty-six months. Their odors, aromas, and flavors evolve over time, so what you like best will be based on how mature you like your cheese, but also the season in which the cheese was produced:

- Mountain cheeses produced in the **spring** are produced with milk from herds grazing on very moist pasture with an absence of aromatic herbs and flowers.
- During the **summer**, herds enjoy more abundant and varied diets: their milk is more aromatic and the cheeses they produce have better ripening potential. Take note, however, that not all cheeses can be aged for more than twelve months, because production in the mountains is fraught with problems—adverse weather and storms—unlike lowland production.
- In the **fall**, the herds return from the mountains and, even though the grass is less nutritious, the gentle climate is conducive to the production of very interesting cheeses.
- In the **winter**, animals return to the barn and are fed on hay (i.e. dried summer grasses) and cereals (especially corn). The aromatic richness of the hay depends on where it has been cut. It is possible to find delicious winter cheeses whose flavors truly develop twelve to twenty-four months later.

❖ *You will be able to find excellent cooked pressed cheeses if you pay attention to when they were made and how long they were matured.*

WHEN IT IS BEST TO TASTE THE 45 AOP CHEESES

THE BEST IN SPRING

Banon - Beaufort - Bleu d'Auvergne - Bleu du Vercors-Sassenage - Brie de Melun
Brocciu, or Brocciu Corse - Cantal - Chabichou du Poitou - Charolais
Chavignol, or Crottin de Chavignol - Chevrotin - Comté - Laguiole - Mâconnais - Ossau-Iraty
Pélardon - Picodon - Pouligny-Saint-Pierre - Rigotte de Condrieu - Rocamadour
Sainte-Maure-de-Touraine - Salers - Selles-sur-Cher - Valençay

THE BEST IN SUMMER

Banon - Beaufort - Bleu de Gex Haut-Jura, or Bleu de Septmoncel - Bleu des Causses
Bleu du Vercors-Sassenage - Brie de Meaux - Brocciu, or Brocciu Corse
Camembert de Normandie - Cantal - Chabichou du Poitou - Chaource
Charolais - Chavignol, or Crottin de Chavignol - Chevrotin
Comté - Époisses - Fourme d'Ambert - Fourme de Montbrison - Laguiole
Mâconnais - Maroilles - Morbier - Munster, or Munster-Géromé - Neufchâtel
Ossau-Iraty - Pélardon - Picodon - Pouligny-Saint-Pierre - Reblochon de Savoie
Rigotte de Condrieu - Rocamadour - Saint-Nectaire - Sainte-Maure-de-Touraine
Salers - Selles-sur-Cher - Tome des Bauges - Valençay

THE BEST IN FALL

Abondance - Banon - Beaufort - Bleu d'Auvergne
Bleu de Gex Haut-Jura, or Bleu de Septmoncel - Bleu des Causses - Bleu du Vercors-Sassenage -
Brie de Meaux - Brocciu, or Brocciu Corse - Camembert de Normandie - Cantal
Chabichou du Poitou - Chaource - Charolais - Chavignol, or Crottin de Chavignol
Chevrotin - Comté - Époisses - Fourme d'Ambert - Fourme de Montbrison - Laguiole
Langres - Mâconnais - Maroilles - Mont d'Or, or Vacherin du Haut-Doubs - Morbier
Munster, or Munster-Géromé - Neufchâtel - Ossau-iraty - Pélardon - Picodon
Pouligny-Saint-Pierre - Reblochon de Savoie - Rigotte de Condrieu - Rocamadour
Roquefort - Saint-Nectaire - Sainte-Maure-de-Touraine - Salers - Selles-sur-Cher
Tome des Bauges - Valençay

THE BEST IN WINTER

Abondance - Beaufort - Bleu d'Auvergne - Bleu de Gex Haut-Jura, or Bleu de Septmoncel
Brie de Meaux - Brie de Melun - Brocciu, or Brocciu Corse - Camembert de Normandie
Cantal - Comté - Époisses - Fourme d'Ambert - Fourme de Montbrison - Laguiole
Maroilles - Mont d'Or, or Vacherin du Haut-Doubs - Munster, or Munster-Géromé
Roquefort - Salers - Tome des Bauges

The Definition of Good Cheese

Some say that a good cheese is an edible cheese; others favor flavor. Today, cheese bacteria are monitored so rigorously that health risks are practically zero. Raw cheese is subject to even greater inspection, which is paradoxical because raw milk contains microorganisms capable of fighting potentially undesirable germs. From a gastronomic perspective, who gets to decide whether a cheese is good or bad? France has developed a rigorous approach to cheese quality: there are the AOP cheese federations that define guidelines for their production and have drawn up a tasting guide for assessment purposes, *Le Guide de dégustation du concours général agricole*, which helps consumers evaluate cheeses. The federations guarantee the flavor tradition. Otherwise, you can always ask your cheesemonger.

Did you know?
The federations' "sensorial evaluation" guidelines govern not only the smell and flavor of cheese but also its texture to the touch and its appearance. Cheese tasting elicits all the senses.

Experiencing Cheese through the Nose

Most of the taste of cheese comes via the nose rather than the taste buds. Savoring the aroma of cheese does not only mean smelling its odor; when we put food in our mouths to taste, the nose is actually doing most of the work in a process called retronasal olfaction. The temperature of the mouth, our chewing action, and the butterfat melting into our saliva release the volatile aromas from the cheese. This stimulates our olfactory receptors, i.e. our sense of smell. What are these aromas? And what words are used to describe them? Aromas can have very emotional associations, so does the cheese world pinpoint, classify, and appraise them in a more scientific way?

Readily recognizable aromas emerge such as cream, fresh mushroom, baker's yeast, ripe fruits, caramel, toasted notes, hay, vanilla, milky coffee, and many more besides. Science speaks of esters, lactones, and methanethiol. Both approaches work; it all depends on who you are talking to.

Did you know?
- A scent or odor is detected in the nose.
- An aroma is what is detected by the nose when the cheese is on the palate.
- Flavors are released on the taste buds. When we speak of flavors, we refer to the five basic flavors detected by the palate: sweet, salty, acid, bitter, or umami.

If a cheese emanates the following odors or these aromas exist, it is generally not a good sign:

- ammonia
- rancidness
- rotting
- bitterness
- oxidation
- grease
- soap
- sourness
- mold
- fermentation
- charring

Other aromas are very welcome:
- fruit and hazelnuts (Abondance, Comté)
- earthy, mushroom notes (Bries and some blue cheeses)
- milk and leather (ewe's milk and matured cow's milk cheeses)

In cheeses, the overall palette of aromas you'll find are:
- lactic aromas (fresh milk, yogurt, butter)
- plants (hay, damp grass, garlic)
- floral aromas (honey, rose, violet)
- fruit (hazelnut, chestnut, banana)
- toasted aromas (smoked, broiled nuts or grains, coffee)
- animal (stables, countryside, meat stock)
- spice (pepper, nutmeg, mint)
- "sulfurous" aromas (cabbage)
- tart and piquant aromas

Facing page: Louis Record, at home in the village of Sost in the Pyrenees (Department 65). The collection of bells on the mantelpiece were once used by Louis on his cows and ewes. They helped to differentiate the animals, locate them, and scare off potential predators. Louis's hands have fashioned many cheeses, and still do.

Dominique Bouchait's opinion
Cheeses can release very distinct aromas that may be deemed a quality in some cheeses but a flaw in others. We have to learn to judge for ourselves. Just because cheese experts fall in love with a cheese, it does not mean everyone will like it.

Cheese Tasting

Cheeses should be consumed in increasing order of flavor from the gentlest flavors to the more robust. You are advised to begin tasting with a fresh cheese and then move on to stronger flavors and harder textures, finishing with blue cheeses, which are good for the digestion. If you are unsure and no indication has been given, a tasting order is hard to implement. In this case, use color as a guide, tasting the paler cheeses first and moving on to the darker ones.

FOLLOW YOUR NOSE
Begin tasting the cheeses with creamy lactic aromas, and move on to those with earthier mushroom notes, before attacking the tangy, fruity, animal, and spiced cheeses on the platter.

USE YOUR EYES
Thick, hard rinds are readily identifiable from more delicate younger cheeses: start with these fresher cheeses. If several cheeses have similar rinds, look out for their color. Opt for paler rinds to begin with, then move on to darker rinds.

WHAT TO DO IF RINDS HAVE THE SAME THICKNESS AND COLOR
- For **soft rinds and soft cheeses**, look at the color of their interior: cheeses with a lighter-colored interior are generally younger than others. In terms of consistency, taste the firmer cheeses first; these will be younger and often have a heart—a drier, crumbly center—which is not necessarily a downside.
- For **harder and pressed cheeses**, opt for the softer ones first. White crystals within the cheese's hard interior are an indication of age. They are a much sought-after characteristic of mature Cheddar and Comté. The more white crystals there are, the more mature the cheese.

If you come across a cheese selection with spices on the rind and/or in the interior (cumin, chiles, herbs, etc.), eat them last. This type of cheese can dominate the palate and overwhelm any subsequent taste. Leave the blue cheese for the end; it contains *Penicillium*, a fungus that helps digestion.

Facing page: A water source in the mountain. Water is essential to the cheesemaker, for both washing cheeses and refreshing their livestock.

The Right Way to Cut Cheese

Every cheese has its knife! A large blade or wire for large wheels; a cheese slicer for fine curls of dry, parmesan-style cheeses; a spoon for Vacherin Mont d'Or and Cancoillotte; or an open surface blade cheese knife for runny cheeses (like Bries and Camemberts), which prevents the cheese from sticking to the knife.

To keep service simple and limit cutlery, a cheese knife with an open-surface blade and fork-tip is essential. It cuts most cheeses to varying widths and the slices can then be pronged for easy service. Always provide several knives if there are several cheeses in order to keep the sometimes powerful flavors separate.

CHEESE-CUTTING COMMANDMENTS

- Always respect the direction of the cheese's height.
- When the cheese is presented as a whole loaf or wheel (Camembert, Munster, Langres, Livarot, and pyramid or heart-shaped cheeses), cut from the center outward.
- Small round cheeses like Pélardon should be cut in half or into quarters.
- When presented with a slice of cheese, adapt the cut so that everybody is served both nose and rind.

Facing page: This *roquefortaise* cheese cutter enables a cheese too fragile for a cheese knife to be cut from top to bottom.

Bread and Cheese

There is a wide variety of bread—from the traditional baguette to cereal and grain loaves. There is no hard and fast rule about what bread to eat with cheese. Serve what you like and experiment:

- A *pain de campagne,* farmhouse bread, works with all cheeses, from the softest to the most flavorful.
- The typical *baguette* is delicious with soft rinds (Brie de Meaux, Camembert de Normandie, etc.); the creamy softness of the cheese contrasts wonderfully with crusty bread. A wholegrain *baguette* will bring even more flavor.
- Rye bread (*pain de seigle*) is generally eaten with seafood in France, but it is also delicious with blue cheeses: the rye is the perfect complement to their tangy aromas.
- The dried fruit (figs, raisins, etc.) of fruit bread brings a sweet touch to the salty cheese experience and really helps express the pungency of blue cheeses.
- Hazelnut and walnut bread combine well with *fruité* cheeses like Comté, Beaufort, and Tomme des Pyrénées.
- Olive or olive oil bread enhances the lactic aromas of fresh cheeses, whether goat's, cow's or ewe's.

Wine and Cheese

Cheese and wine get on well but are they really "best buddies"? Not always. It has long been thought that cheese should be served with red wine, and some people still go along with this idea. However, with several exceptions, even magnificent red wines can hinder the flavors of cheese. When the tannins in wine encounter the butterfat, rind, and lactic acid bacteria of cheese, they dominate the palate and stifle the aromas of cheese. The result is often bitter and harsh on the tongue, a disappointment for cheese and wine lovers alike.

Pairing Cheese and Wine
Once upon a time, the red wine that farmers made was lighter in color. It was known as *piquette* and contained few tannins. This lighter, fruitier wine did not hinder the flavors of cheese and so the habit stuck and became a tradition.

Facing page: A forest between two peaks, the Col du Soulor and the Col de Spandelles. Many farmstead cheesemakers use wood to heat the milk the day before to raise the temperature of the cut curds.

Cheese and white wine, however, works very well, especially when cheeses are combined with wines from the same *terroir* or region. As a general rule of thumb: Savoie cheeses work well with Savoie wines, Burgundy cheeses with Burgundy wines, etc. For non-wine-producing regions, the regional alcoholic beverage is always somehow perfect: Local cider is great with Camembert de Normandie, for example, and beer is marvelous with Maroilles. There are some exceptions: with blue cheeses such as Roquefort, fortified wines or sweet wines, not necessarily indigenous to the region, are particularly delicious.

Tip

If you are unsure about your cheeses and your wines, try matching colors. It is not by chance that white wines generally suit cheeses better than red.

A matured, straw yellow Comté *fruité* works well with nutty *vin jaune* from the Jura, whereas young Comté works better with a drier white wine.

If you only have red wine, choose cheeses with colored rinds (aged Cantal, Epoisses, Saint-Nectaire, dry goat's cheeses, etc.)—great pairings between certain cheeses and red wines can be found. Cheese and wine pairings are a matter of taste. Develop your own habits and change according to how you feel.

Champagne and Cheese

Champagne with cheese is a pairing I have been experimenting with more, recently, and in conclusion I can safely say: champagne and goat's cheese make for a perfect combination. Champagne with gorgonzola is particularly effective. These are pairings I have begun to offer more frequently for festive occasions or simply as an aperitif: beginning an evening with a glass of champagne and a variety of cheese offerings always meets with great success!

Several successful pairings:

- brut champagne with Brie, Camembert, or mature Salers is a classic pairing
- mature Comté or aged Mimolette work well with vintage champagne
- Livarot, Pont l'Évêque, Maroilles, and Chaource paired with rosé champagne is delicious
- Fourme d'Ambert or Bleu d'Auvergne with a demi-sec or extra-dry champagne is a delicate mouthful

Facing page: Wine, bread, and cheese are a perfect combination. Here, I deliberately included a Langres from the Champagne region.

Composing a Cheese Platter

Cheese platters offer infinite possibilities. A good platter depends on the composition and the way it is presented. A platter should look mouthwatering, enticing curiosity and the desire to indulge.

THE QUANTITIES REQUIRED

First, find out how many guests there will be. If you are serving a platter at the end of a meal, provide between 3½ to 5¼ ounces of cheese per person with five to seven cheeses. If the platter is a main course, as part of a buffet, say, provide 8¾ to 10½ ounces per person, with ten to twelve cheeses or more.

CHOOSING CHEESE

If you are unfamiliar with cheese, trust your cheesemonger and ask the person to select the best and ripest for the date of the event. The cheesemonger will also suggest the order of tasting. Tell the cheesemonger about your requirements: if it is an end of meal platter or a buffet platter. If it is intended for the end of the meal, tell the person your menu, so that he or she can provide continuity in flavors and match your wine list. If it is for a buffet, tell your cheesemonger what the occasion is: a simple aperitif or some other larger festive gathering.

You can also ask your cheesemonger to offer a selection according to a theme, for example:
- seasonal cheeses
- cheeses from the same region (if you are providing for a buffet, try creating several platters from different regions)
- ewe's cheeses (a farmstead Pérail, a Brocciu Passu, a farmstead Ossau-Iraty, a Pecorino, and a Roquefort)
- cooked cheeses (Appenzel, Beaufort, Comté, Gruyère, and Parmesan)
- soft-rind cheeses (Saint-Félicien, Camembert de Normandie, Brie de Melun, Livarot, and, why not, the Belgian cheese, Herve)

Everything is possible and discovering is fascinating!

Cheese Presentation

A very simple method involves classifying by color of rind, from the lightest to the darkest. If the rinds are the same color, sort them by color of the interior or by smell, the gentlest to the most complex.

Avoid positioning cheeses too closely together: they should not touch one another. Find a platter large enough to give each enough room. Too many cheeses on a single platter can be difficult to cut, so use two evenly balanced and elegantly prepared platters rather than a single plate of cheeses where they will be overwhelmed.

> ### *Label the cheeses, too:*
> **It can be frustrating for guests when they love a cheese but do not know its name.**

IDEAS FOR SMALLER OCCASIONS AND GRAND EVENTS

When choosing cheeses, have fun inventing themes:

- For a gathering among family and friends (weddings, birthdays, communions, etc.), create labels celebrating the people involved and place them on their favorite cheeses. Find a cheese from somewhere important to them (their home region, where you met, where they were married) and place that cheese in pride of place in the middle of the platter.
- For an open-air buffet, choose seasonal cheeses and present them with other seasonal produce (for example, in the fall, serve pears, raisins, and walnuts).
- For a romantic tête-à-tête, decorate your platter with the food of love! A goat's cheese sprinkled with hot chile, a Comté served with a glass of champagne, a Fourme d'Ambert accompanied by raisins soaked in sweet sauternes wine . . . the ideas are endless.
- For small budgets, check your cheesemonger's selection carefully—you will always find several options at affordable prices: Cantal, Bleu de Gex, Morbier, Tome des Bauges, Camembert or blue Fourmes.

Always taste from lightest to strongest!

Spring	Summer
●	●

From top to bottom: Cabécou, Mignon de Brébis, Pouligny-Saint-Pierre, Reblochon, Pont l'Évêqu, Salers, Ossau-Iraty, and César Régalis ewe's milk blue cheese.

Caillaou d'Escanecrabe (a raw milk goat's cheese), ewe's milk Ricochet, Corsican Tomme, Échourgnac, Cheddar, butter with Espelette pepper, goat's milk blue cheese.

Always taste from lightest to strongest!

Fall	Winter
—◆—	—◆—

Charolais, two *barattes* of goat's cheese, fresh crottin of goat's cheese, Neufchâtel, Napoléon Commingeois, Livarot, Langres, Boulette d'Avesnes, and Bleu de Gex Haut-Jura.

Tour du Montot (a goat's cheese), Morbier, Comté aged for 24 months, Maroilles, Epoisses de Bourgogne, Roquefort, Shropshire Blue.

Butter and Cheese

Yes, I frequently include butter (raw milk butter, of course) on my platters. It is a marvelous flavor enhancer. Try aged Comté on bread and butter—it's magnificent.

Cooking with Cheese

All cheeses can be cooked but each in its own way. Fresh cheeses are perfect for sauces and stuffing because they help bind them. Drier cheeses work perfectly with gratins and soups for the gooey, stringy texture they bring.

When cooking cheese for a fondue, it is important to melt the cheese on a low heat, otherwise the fats will separate and you will be left with a pot of hot butter-fat!

Combining Cheeses with Other Dishes

Back in the days when cheese production was not yet a refined art, mistakes were common. If the flavor was too strong and sharp, cheeses were eaten with bread, wine, and even preserves.

> ### The Tale of Aligot
> Long ago, in humble households where meat was scarce, cheese provided flavor and sustenance at family mealtimes, where it was served with soup and potatoes. Cheese was made the focal point of the dish: *Aligot* is a typical example. *Aligot* originates in the mountainous remote volcanic regions of the Auvergne, Aubrac, and Lozère in central France. Its name comes from the Latin *aliquod*, which prosaically means "something to eat."
> When pilgrims set out on the Way of Saint James, they would knock at monastery doors and ask for *aliquid*. They were served a thin soup containing bread and crumbs of fresh tomme cheese. Over time food habits changed and the bread was replaced by potatoes.

Cheese is obviously an important player in a number of well-known dishes—pizzas, gratins, salads, and pasta —where it is used to provide texture, to bind ingredients together, or to enhance flavor. Today cheese accompanies other dishes, especially for the flavors and textures it brings, often providing new taste sensations or a touch of originality to familiar classics.

Facing page (top to bottom):
Raw milk butter from Bresse, Isigny, and Charentes-Poitou.

CHEESE AND HEALTH

Although it is an integral part of French daily food habits, cheese is often accused of containing too much salt and fat. The diktats of waistline but also food allergies, lactose intolerance, cholesterol issues, and the raw-milk listeria scare form a long list of charges for any food suspect. Is cheese totally risk free? Is it as fattening as people say? Can we trust labels? Is listeria to be feared?

Is cheese good for health?

Cheese is rich in nutrients and micronutrients—proteins with essential amino acids, vitamins A and B, calcium, minerals . . . but these differ from one cheese to another:

- Fat content varies from 0 to 1¾ ounces/3½ ounces, depending on the fat content of the milk or cream used.
- Calcium content is related to draining conditions: the most calcium-rich are cooked pressed cheeses (Parmesan: .04 ounce/3.5 ounces; Emmental: .03 ounce/3.5 ounces; Beaufort: .02 ounce/3.5 ounces). For example, a two-year-old Parmesan cheese requires almost 5¼ gallons of milk for 2¼ pounds of cheese, as opposed to 2¾ gallons for other cheeses.
- Matured cheeses are high in group B vitamins (B2, B9) and higher-fat cheeses are high in vitamin A. Again, everything depends on the type of milk used to create the cheese.

TEETH

In tests on human subjects, it has been observed that cheese consumption prevents tooth decay (in a study by the Centre National Interprofessionnel de l'Economie Laitière [CNIEL], the French dairy professionals' federation). It was found that the minerals contained in cheese—especially calcium and phosphorus—contribute to the mineralization of teeth while also preventing their demineralization. Further more, chewing cheese activates the secretion of saliva and helps reduce acidity in the mouth after consuming sugars, which also combats tooth decay.

It has been proven that cheeses made from milk fermented by lactic acid bacteria (Langres, Munster, goat's cheeses, etc.) contain properties that stimulate the immune system. These bacteria colonize in our intestinal flora, and they have a protective effect. Foods containing lactic acid bacteria should be consumed on a regular basis to enjoy their full benefits.

DIABETES PREVENTION
According to recent studies, high levels of milk and dairy product consumption are associated with a reduced risk of type-2 diabetes. This protection is provided by its calcium and magnesium content, two minerals that increase sensitivity to insulin and glucose tolerance. Whey proteins may also help control blood-sugar levels.
❖ *Everything is a question of balance, in cheese as in the rest of life: moderation in everything. According to age, weight, and state of health, everybody should adapt the amount of cheese they eat.*

Low-Salt Cheeses

Zero-salt cheese does not exist, but there are low-salt cheeses such as Gouda, Comté, and Gruyère. In the last few years, the range of this type of product has greatly increased given the number of people tied to a low-salt diet.
Among the cheeses with the lowest sodium content are (from the least salty to the saltiest): fromage frais and fromage blanc; Saint-Marcellin (natural soft rind); Brie de Meaux (soft cheese, bloomy rind); Munster (pressed cheese, washed rind).

Contra-Indications

Cheese can be contra-indicated, but this should only come from your doctor. Your doctor will establish how much cheese it is safe to eat for you and your condition. High-cholesterol and obesity are two such conditions where a doctor will impose restrictions on fat consumption.

Raw Milk Cheese: is it Unhealthy and Even Dangerous?

Raw milk cheeses do not always have a good reputation, especially when it comes to pregnancy (see the following question). However, the lactic acid bacteria that they contain are excellent for our intestinal flora. It is worth stating once and for all: raw milk cheeses pose no more problems for health than pasteurized cheeses, because the balance in their natural bacteria autoimmunizes them and they are actually able to resist dangerous pathogens such as listeria.

Furthermore after affinage, raw milk cheeses have a better ability to ward off problematic pathogens than pasteurized cheeses, because pasteurized cheeses do not benefit from the immunity provided by the vast scope of bacterial defenses of raw milk cheeses.

❖ *Raw milk cheeses are no more dangerous than others. They simply take longer and are more expensive to produce because of the many hygiene tests they have to undergo, and the complex skills required to manufacture and mature them.*

Raw Milk Cheese and Pregnancy

It is generally not recommended to eat raw milk cheeses when pregnant, especially soft rind and bloomy rind cheeses such as Camembert or Brie, because there is an outside chance they may contain harmful bacteria. Soft cheeses like these are more open to bacterial contamination than hard cheeses. If matured for more than six months, hard cheeses can be safely consumed during pregnancy. You can thus enjoy anything from Gruyère to Parmesan, Cheddar to Comté. To be on the safe side, however, you are advised not to eat the rind.

Did you know?
Cooked cheese carries zero risk of bacterial contamination. So if you feel an urge for bloomy rind or raw milk cheeses, cook them well and you can indulge to your heart's content. Listeria is destroyed at temperatures above 158°F. Be aware: this does not mean simply melting a cheese but actually cooking it. The cheese should be oozing and creamy to the center and have a golden crust. You can tuck into gratins, baked Camemberts, and traditional, hearty tartiflettes (see recipes) to your heart's content!

Listeria

When anybody mentions raw milk cheese, people are most afraid of listeria. What people do not realize, however, is that the diversity of bacteria in raw milk is the key factor preventing the development of listeria. *Consortia microbiens* bacteria, especially, play an important autoimmunizing role. The health risk is thus low, despite health scares of the past.

All cheese professionals remember the famous 1987 listeria outbreak caused by a Vacherin Mont d'Or Suisse, which caused thirty-four deaths due to listeria. The listeria bacteria itself was not present in the milk and did not develop during manufacture but during maturation in the caves d'affinage. Furthermore, the milk was not raw but thermized, which partly explains why it became contaminated. In the thermizing process, the protective bacteria of milk are killed and so it is unable to defend itself against listeria.

In 2010, in its study of the semi-soft, washed rind cheese, Saint-Nectaire, the French international agricultural research centre (INRA) found that the level of bacteria naturally present in cheese helps to actively combat listeria (detailed in the paper "Sécurité sanitaire et qualités sensorielles. La biodiversité microbienne au service des cheeses au raw milk," [Health Safety and Taste Quality. Bacterial Biodiversity and raw-milk cheeses] April 2010).

If this collection of bacteria is separated out, the development of listeria increases. The study was carried out in comparison to commercial dairy products unpro-

Facing page: (left) Four cheesemakers in fine health. From left to right, Corine Boucheron and her daughter Coralie Fourcadet-Vaz, with Christiane Duplan and her daughter Nelly Duplan, and four of the littlest family members. *(right)* Mrs. Espoune and her daughter. The family has been making cheese for several generations.

FAT CONTENT OF AOP CHEESES

AOP CHEESE	% OF TOTAL WEIGHT
↓	↓

FRESH CHEESES

Brocciu, or Brocciu Corse	8 %

SOFT CHEESES WITH NATURAL RIND

Chabichou du Poitou	25 %
Charolais	31 %
Chavignol, or Crottin de Chavignol	31 %
Mâconnais	29 %
Pélardon	28 %
Picodon	29 %
Pouligny-Saint-Pierre	28 %
Rigotte de Condrieu	20 %
Rocamadour	23 %
Sainte-Maure-de-Touraine	24 %
Selles-sur-Cher	29 %
Valençay	29 %

SOFT CHEESES WITH WASHED RIND

Époisses	23 %
Langres	23 %
Livarot	22 %
Maroilles	29 %
Mont d'Or, or Vacherin du Haut-Doubs	23 %
Munster, or Munster-Géromé	23 %
Pont-l'évêque	24 %

SOFT CHEESES WITH BLOOMY RIND

Banon	*25%*
Brie de Meaux	*22%*
Brie de Melun	*23%*
Camembert de Normandie	*22%*
Chaource	*24%*
Neufchâtel	*22%*

COOKED PRESSED CHEESES

Beaufort	*32%*
Comté	*33%*

PRESSED SEMI-COOKED CHEESES

Abondance	*32%*

UNCOOKED PRESSED CHEESES

Cantal	*30%*
Chevrotin	*23%*
Laguiole	*30%*
Morbier	*28%*
Ossau-iraty	*34%*
Reblochon de Savoie	*26%*
Saint-nectaire	*28%*
Salers	*28%*
Tome des Bauges	*26%*

BLUE CHEESES

Bleu d'Auvergne	*28%*
Bleu de Gex Haut-Jura, or Bleu de Septmoncel	*29%*
Bleu des Causses	*29%*
Bleu du Vercors-Sassenage	*28%*
Fourme d'Ambert	*27%*
Fourme de Montbrison	*27%*

tected by this bacterial shield. The commercial products were invaded by the listeria bacteria.

Unfortunately we are still unable to artificially reproduce the microbial floras that develop during maturation on the rinds of raw milk cheeses in order to create controlled alternatives.

Fat Content and Cheese

Before 2007, cheese labels indicated the fat content of cheese in relation to dry weight, i.e. what remained of the product after the total removal of water. Since 2007, by law, cheese labels have to mention the total fat content in relationship to the product's total weight, including its water content, a much more consumer-friendly approach that makes it easier for consumers to compare the fat content of various cheeses.

The former regulations were highly misleading. A fresh cheese labeled 40% fat actually contains half the fat of a pressed cheese with the same fat to solid-matter ratio. Where a fresh cheese contains 80% water, which means only 8% fat of its total weight, a pressed cheese contains less than 40% water, meaning a higher fat ratio.

- The more water a cheese contains the lower the fat content.
- Fresh cheeses contain the most water (approximately 80%).
- Soft rind cheeses contain between 50 to 55% water.
- Semi-hard cheeses contain approximately 45% water.
- Hard cheeses contain 35% water.

Did you know?
One of the cheeses with the lowest fat content is Cancoillotte with 6% fat.

While the fat to total-weight ratio is not indicated on the cheese, you should refer to the table of nutritional contents. Fat content is indicated per 3½ ounces of cheese: ¼ ounce of fat corresponds to 8% of the total weight. *Fermier* cheeses are exempt from this ruling as the precise fat content depends on *affinage*, so the phrase "matière grasse non précisée" (unspecified fat content) may be found.

The Healthiest Milk

All milk is composed of water, fat, carbohydrates, minerals, and vitamins. The milk with the highest calorie count is ewe's milk, due to its high fat content. This fat is made up of shorter fatty acid chains than cow's milk, which makes it easier to digest. It is also high in calcium, zinc, group B vitamins, and phosphorus.

Goat's milk has a reputation for being healthy; it is the milk most similar to human milk. Goat's milk is often more digestible than cow's milk and is good for our intestinal flora. High in minerals and vitamins A and B3, it is an important energy source. In his *Essays,* Michel de Montaigne wrote: "It is commonplace here, when women of the village cannot feed their children from their breasts, to see them call upon goats for succor."

MILK ALLERGIES

Allergies to milk proteins are becoming more common among children under two, but there is no reason to think that goat's milk or cow's milk proteins react any differently and neither presents any specific particularities.

Cheese and Digestion

Problems digesting cheese could be due to a food allergy or milk intolerance. The two components of cheese that could cause digestive problems are lactose (carbohydrate) and casein (protein). But unlike milk and butter, cheese is a fermented product, which means it contains little or no lactose.

LACTOSE-FREE

During the digestive process, lactose is broken down by an enzyme, lactase, to form lactic acid. This is known as lactic fermentation (see page 27).

Hard and semihard cooked cheeses do not contain lactose, as most of the carbohydrate drains into the whey during the cheese-manufacturing process. The rest is entirely broken down during *affinage,* which means that hard cheeses can be eaten by the lactose intolerant.

Dates on Cheese Labels

There is usually one or the other: a "use by" date (DLC) or a "best before" date (DDM).

• The **date limite de consommation** (DLC) is more specific than the Anglophone "use by" or "sell by" labels and applies to potentially harmful foodstuffs like eggs, shellfish, and dairy produce. According to EU law, the DLC applies to "perishable items likely to present an immediate danger to consumers' health after a short period of time." This means that after the DLC, the product could give rise to digestive issues or food poisoning.

• The **date de durabilité minimale** (DDM) is similar to the "best before" date. These dates are advisory. A cheese can still be consumed after the DDM has passed; its flavor, odor, and texture might be compromised however.

Cheese and Diet

In France, cheese is part of the national gastronomic heritage and it is difficult to imagine a meal without cheese. To avoid weight gain with cheese, remember this: the denser a cheese (e.g. Comté, Beaufort, etc.), the higher the concentration of milk, so the higher the butterfat content—these cheeses contain less water. A creamy cheese, however, has less fat because it contains more water.

❖ *Nutritional experts agree: cheese when consumed in moderation as part of a balanced diet does not make you fat. You just have to adapt the quantities depending on the type of cheese.*

UNUSUAL QUESTIONS ABOUT CHEESE

I have been asked so many odd cheese-related questions in my career that I have made a collection of the most frequently asked, plus one or two that made me smile.

Why Don't all Cheeses Smell the Same?

Cheese is made up of lactic matter and bacteria, which give off characteristic odors. All bacteria create their own distinct aromas, so every cheese will be different. A cheese's rind is predominantly made up of bacteria and mold, so a cheese's flavors and aromas concentrate especially in this layer.

Why Do People from Alsace in the East Eat Unripe Munster and People from Normandy Eat Unripe Camembert?

The characteristics of these particular cheeses come from the development on their rind of microscopic Penicillin-type molds (*Penicillium albumou camemberti* in Camembert, for example). These molds develop during the cheese-ripening process: early in their development, they are white and gradually grow darker in color to give the cheese its final color. The storage and transport times required to ship Munster and Camembert from their production regions to their points of sale mean that cheeses evolve. If in their regions local people are consuming local cheeses with pale rinds, it is because fresher cheeses are more readily available at home.

Why is Butter Yellow and Milk White?

Butter is essentially made from milk fat. The more water is removed through heat, the darker the color of butter becomes: from white it turns ivory then pale yellow. While butter's natural color is yellow, the intensity of the yellow depends on the milk's origin. This color comes from carotene, an orange pigment naturally present in the plant matter eaten by cows in their diets of grass, hay, silage, seeds, and cereals. When absorbed into the digestive system, carotene is transformed into vitamin A.

The color of butter depends on what cows eat. In summer, butter is often darker than the rest of the year, because their grass diet is high in carotene and chlorophyll. In order to conserve the same color year-round, carotene or another natural pigment is sometimes added to butter to give it that appealing vivid yellow color. On the packaging, these added pigments appear as colorants.

Why Do Some Cheeses Have Holes?

During affinage, cheeses such as Emmental are matured at higher temperatures to create cavities, known as "eyes," in the interior. Heat favors the development of certain bacteria, which then release bubbles of carbon dioxide (CO_2) responsible for the holes in the interior. The thickness of the rinds of cheeses "with holes" is so thick that it prevents this carbon dioxide escaping: the bubbles produced grow larger and multiply. The affineur is able to control the size and quantity of the "eyes." When there are enough, the cheese is returned to lower temperatures and the bacteria go to sleep and cease their CO_2 production.

Why do these "eyes" sometimes cry?
During affinage, as the cheese ages, the salt added during manufacture forms back into crystals. These salt crystals then begin to draw out any remaining water, producing "teary eyes", a state that tells the cheese lover they are in the presence of a cheese at its optimum quality.

Following spread (left): A block of raw-milk butter already opened; (right): A slice of Emmental. Due to the extra fermentation, an interior with holes will have more flavor than an interior without.

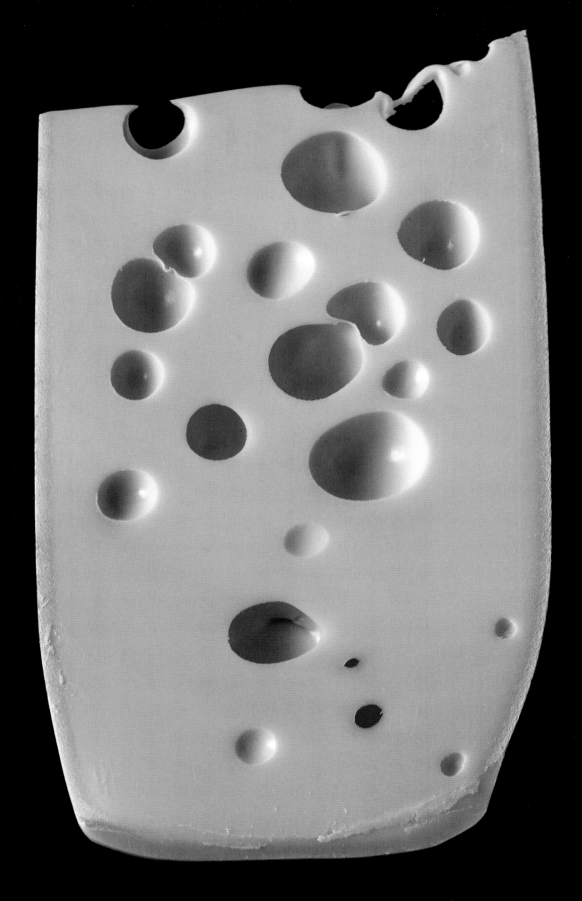

Why Do People Try To Catch Mice With Cheese?

Because the aroma of cheese attracts mice. The best cheeses to catch mice are Comté, Gruyère, and Reblochon. Mice are less fond of blue or soft, alcohol-washed rinds, no doubt because of their odor. Mice are not actually that crazy about cheese, however, and its appeal ends with its aroma, contrary to popular belief. Mice love carbs, such as cereals, bread, and even paper. If you really want to treat a mouse, save your aged Comté and simply get yourself a cat!

> *Did you know?*
> **Pigeon lovers add cheese to their homing pigeons' diets to build up their energy after long flights. They also feed them whey to help the birds eliminate toxins built up during the muscular activity involved in flying.**

Why Are There Big White Spots in Old Cheeses?

When a cheese ages, it loses its water and the dry matter becomes more concentrated; when a cheese made for long preservation has aged sufficiently, white flecks appear. These are known as cheese crystals, formed when amino acids break down to form crystals. It is a sign of quality. These white spots are to be found on Swiss Gruyère, Beaufort, and Parmesan. The older a cheese is, the more white crystals you will find.

Why Is Comté Never Fermier When Cantal Is?

A *fermier*, or farmstead, cheese is a cheese made with the milk of a single herd (see page 57). Instead of farmsteads, Comté has *fruitières*, formerly known as *fructeries* when they first appeared in the thirteenth century. *Fruitières* are places where farmers take their udder-fresh milk every day to be ripened. Combining milks this way enables the creation of cheeses large enough for winter preservation. This cooperative community spirit has survived industrialization today.

And in the interests of quality and tradition, *fruitière* production has become a condition of AOP status. AOP Comté regulations state that milk must be transported directly after milking to the place of production. Renneting must occur within twenty-four hours. The milk may be heated once at the renneting stage. Salt or brine must be applied directly to the surface. The casein label must be applied to the side of the cheese. And grated cheese may not be sold as Comté.

If Comté is not a *fermier* cheese, it is perhaps because of its unusual mountain

Facing page: Parmesan aged for thirty months with cheese crystals. Cheese crystals are often found on cooked pressed cheeses.

location. In the Jura region, the slopes are steep and the houses close together so it is easier to pool the fruits of ones labor. In the Cantal region in central France, on the contrary, farms are farther apart, encouraging a farmstead approach.

Why Is Mimolette Orange?

The color of Mimolette comes from a natural pigment, called "annatto," which is very often used in the food industry—in cheese, sausages, cold drinks, and butter, etc. Annatto is extracted from the fruit of the achiote, a tree that grows in Central and South America, India, and Africa. The fruit is inedible. It is harvested then dried to extract the wax around the seeds. The seeds are very high in carotene, which gives Mimolette its orange color. Annatto has a whole range of different colors from pale yellow to dark orange.

Did you know?
Not only is Mimolette orange, but some producers also dye their cheeses green, red, and blue, depending on the coloring agent they use. This apparently makes for a more festive cheese platter. Each to his or her own.

Why Is There "Caramel" Is Some Cheeses?

The "caramel" we talk about in relation to cheese has nothing to do with candy and cakes. "Caramel" in cheese is a brown coloring agent used for its visual appeal: it enhances the natural ochre hues of the rind and makes them more uniform across the surface. By law it has to be indicated on cheese labels as "E150a," but its use is widespread within the industry.

Facing page: A small cheese *cave d'affinage* belonging to a single farmstead containing ten cows and a unique cheese-making tradition. This is why there are more than fourteen hundred raw milk cheeses in France.

What Do The Colored Labels On Some Cheeses Mean?

In the milk industry, some cheeses are identified using casein labels of different shapes and colors depending on the cheeses. They are set in place during manufacture and are a guarantee of authenticity. They are distributed to producers by AOP management bodies and enable cheeses to be traced:

•All **Reblochons** are identifiable by a green or red disk issued by the Reblochon producers' syndicate. The disk is placed on one side of the cheese and features the production workshop number. The disk is red for dairy cheeses and green for *fermier* reblochons.

• The **Beaufort** has a blue oval casein label identifying the production workshop as well as the day and month of manufacture.

• **Saint-Nectaire** has a green casein label but its shape varies according to its production—it is oval for *fermier* Saint-Nectaire and square for dairy Saint-Nectaire. The plate always includes the departmental number and a series of figures identifying the producer and village where the product was produced as well as the specific batch number of the cheese itself.

Can Cheese Be Taken to the Moon?

In 1996, seventeen Picodons were sent into space with a French astronaut taking part in a seventeen-day American space mission. The cheese with the most space travel experience is Parmesan (or Parmigiano Reggiano), the famous Italian AOP cow's milk cheese. Why Parmesan? Because its structure resists an absence of gravity. Its maiden space voyage took place in 1996 with the Italian astronauts, Cheli and Guidoni, on board the Columbia space shuttle. Then in 2000 it returned on board the Mir space station, where it was stored in one-ounce portions in modified atmospheric conditions.

Apart from its especially robust structure, as an item of food Parmesan is exemplary. It is highly digestible and highly stable due to its long aging process of eighteen, twenty-two, thirty-six, and even forty-eight months. This makes Parmesan the go-to cheese for astronauts. What's more it is high in calcium and provides a readily assimilable source of the mineral, which, in zero gravity, is lost by the skeleton. In 2005, it became part of the official food supply for all astronauts on the International Space Station.

Facing page: Here the sun is a late riser. The herds will be sent to the other side of the mountain where grass and sunlight are plentiful.

THE
AOP
CHEESES

Today there are forty-five cheeses in France with the AOP label, guaranteeing consumers the authentic quality and flavor specific to traditional production methods. (The numbers in parentheses refer to the number of the French department.)

1	*Maroilles*	Aisne (02) and Nord (59)
2	*Neufchâtel*	Seine-Maritime (76) and Oise (60)
3	*Pont l'Évêque*	Calvados (14), Eure (27), Manche (50), and Orne (61)
4	*Livarot*	Calvados (14), Eure (27) and Orne (61)
5	*Camembert de Normandie*	Calvados (14), Eure (27), Manche (50) and Orne (61)
6	*Brie de Meaux*	Aube (10), Loiret (45), Marne (51), Haute-Marne (52), Meuse (55), Seine-et-Marne (77) and Yonne (89)
7	*Brie de Melun*	Aube (10), Seine-et-Marne (77) and Yonne (89)
8	*Chaource*	
9	*Langres*	Côte-d'Or (21), Haute-Marne (52) and Vosges (88)
10	*Munster, or Munster-Géromé*	Bas-Rhin (67), Haut-Rhin (68), Haute-Saône (70), Meurthe-et-Moselle (54), Moselle (57), Vosges (88) and Territoire de Belfort (90)
11	*Selles-sur-Cher*	Cher (18), Indre (36) and Loir-et-Cher (41)
12	*Chavignol, or Crottin de Chavignol*	Cher (18), Loiret (45) and Nièvre (58)
13	*Sainte-Maure-de-Touraine*	Indre (36), Indre-et-Loire (37), Loir-et-Cher (41) and Vienne (86)
14	*Valençay*	Cher (18), Indre (36), Indre-et-Loire (37) and Loir-et-Cher (41)
15	*Mont d'Or, or Vacherin du Haut-Doubs*	Doubs (25)
16	*Epoisses*	Côte-d'Or (21), Haute-Marne (52) and Yonne (89)
17	*Morbier*	Ain (01), Doubs (25), Jura (39) and Saône-et-Loire (71)
18	*Chabichou du Poitou*	Charente (16), Deux-Sèvres (79) and Vienne (86)
19	*Pouligny-Saint-Pierre*	Indre (36)
20	*Comté*	Ain (01), Doubs (25), Haute-Savoie (74), Jura (39) and Saône-et-Loire (71)
21	*Mâconnais*	Rhône (69) and Saône-et-Loire (71)
22	*Bleu de Gex Haut-Jura, or Bleu de Septmoncel*	Ain (01) and Jura (39)
23	*Charolais*	Allier (03), Loire (42), Rhône (69) and Saône-et-Loire (71)
24	*Abondance*	Haute-Savoie (74)
25	*Fourme de Montbrison*	Cantal (15), Loire (42) and Puy-de-Dôme (63)
26	*La fourme de Montbrison*	Loire (42) and Puy-de-Dôme (63)
27	*Reblochon de Savoie*	Savoie (73) and Haute-Savoie (74)
28	*Saint-Nectaire*	Cantal (15) and Puy-de-Dôme (63)
29	*Chevrotin*	Savoie (73) and Haute-Savoie (74)
30	*Bleu d'Auvergne*	Aveyron (12), Cantal (15), Corrèze (19), Haute-Loire (43), Lot (46), Lozère (48) and Puy-de-Dôme (63)
31	*Rigotte de Condrieu*	Loire (42) and Rhône (69)
32	*Tome des Bauges*	Savoie (73) and Haute-Savoie (74)
33	*Beaufort*	Savoie (73) and Haute-Savoie (74)
34	*Salers*	Aveyron (12), Cantal (15), Corrèze (19), Haute-Loire (43) and Puy-de-Dôme (63)
35	*Cantal*	Aveyron (12), Cantal (15), Corrèze (19), Haute-Loire (43) and Puy-de-Dôme (63)
36	*Picodon*	Ardèche (07), Drôme (26), Gard (30) and Vaucluse (84)
37	*Bleu du Vercors-Sassenage*	Drôme (26) and Isère (38)
38	*Rocamadour*	Aveyron (12), Corrèze (19), Dordogne (24), Lot (46) and Tarn-et-Garonne (82)
39	*Laguiole*	Aveyron (12), Cantal (15) and Lozère (48)
40	*Banon*	Alpes-de-Haute-Provence (04), Hautes-Alpes (05), Drôme (26) and Vaucluse (84)
41	*Bleu des Causses*	Aveyron (12), Lot (46), Lozère (48), Gard (30) and Hérault (34)
42	*Roquefort*	Aude (11), Aveyron (12), Gard (30), Hérault (34), Lozère (48) and Tarn (8)
43	*Pélardon*	Aude (11), Gard (30), Hérault (34), Lozère (48) and Tarn (81)
44	*Ossau-Iraty*	Hautes-Pyrénées (65) and Pyrénées-Atlantiques (64)
45	*Brocciu, or Brocciu Corse*	Corse du Sud (2A) and Haute-Corse (2B)

North Sea

English Channel

Maroilles **1**

2 Neufchâtel

NORD - PAS DE CALAIS
PICARDIE

3 Pont l'Évêque

Livarot **4**

5 Camembert
de Normandie

6 Brie de Meaux

NORMANDIE

ÎLE DE FRANCE

ALSACE - CHAMPAGNE
ARDENNES - LORRAINE

BRETAGNE

Brie de Melun **7**

Seine

PAYS DE LA LOIRE

CENTRE
VAL-DE-LOIRE

Chaource **8**

9 Langres

Munster **10**

VOSGES

Rhin

BOURGOGNE
FRANCHE-COMTÉ

Loire

Chavignol

Selles-sur-cher **11**   **12**

Mont d'Or **15**

Sainte-Maure-de-Touraine **13**

14

16 Époisses

Morbier **17**

Comté **20**

Atlantic Ocean

Chabichou **18**
du Poitou

19 Pouligny-Saint-Pierre

21 Mâconnais

JURA

Charolais **23**

Bleu de Gex **22**

24 Abondance

N

Chevrotin **29**

27 Reblochon

Fourme d'Ambert **25**

26 Fourme
de Montbrison

32 Tome des Bauges

Saint-Nectaire **28**

31 Rigotte
de Condrieu

33 Beaufort

Bleu d'Auvergne **30**

MASSIF
CENTRAL

Salers **34**

35 Cantal

36 Picodon

37 Le Bleu
du Vercors-Sassenage

AQUITAINE
LIMOUSIN
POITOU-CHARENTES

AUVERGNE
RHÔNE-ALPES

ALPES

38 Rocamadour

39 Laguiole

Rhône

40 Banon

LANGUEDOC-ROUSSILLON
MIDI-PYRÉNÉES

Garonne

41 Bleu des Causses

PROVENCE-ALPES
CÔTE-D'AZUR

42 Roquefort

43 Pélardon

44 Ossau-Iraty

PYRÉNÉES

Mediterranean Sea

45 Brocciu

CORSE

125

ABONDANCE AOC 1990

◆

**Pressed
Semi-cooked**

SEASON

SPRING   SUMMER   FALL   WINTER

○ *Geography and Origin:* During the Hundred Years' War in the 1400s, the monks of the Abbey of Abondance adopted a breed of cattle suitable for the local landscape. This breed, Abondance, enabled them to develop grazing on prairies and *alpages* and to create the eponymous cheese. Its flavor was found to be so exceptional that during the Papal Conclave in Avignon in 1378, before electing the new pope, Urbain VI, the priests were said to have held off their decision until they had finished the ton of cheese they had ordered to celebrate the occasion. Today, among all French AOP cheeses, Abondance is the only pressed semi-cooked cheese. Its AOP regulations state that it can only be made with cow's milk of the Abondance, Tarine, or Montbeliard breeds.

○ *Choose the Best:* Abondance is a flat cheese with a concave heel, never more than 2¾ to 3¼ inches high. Its rind, which should not have black spots, ranges from golden yellow to brown. The rind is created using a *morge* wash, a brine solution containing cheese bacteria that gives the rind its canvas-like appearance. The interior is supple, even pliable, but not elastic, with an ivory to pale yellow color. If the cheese looks white, firm, and hard, with large cracks, the quality is poor. If, however, it has small regular, well-distributed holes, or "eyes," it is probably very good. Abondance is known for its slightly bitter taste with nutty aromas. It should never be astringent or sweet. Its texture should be pliable, never hard, floury, or granular.

○ *How to Serve:* While Abondance is classically served at the end of the meal, it can also be served as a "Berthoud," a typical Savoie dish: layer small ramekins with thin slices of Abondance, then cover with Savoie white wine. Bake for ten minutes in the oven and you are in for a real feast.

/ ☞ / Its closest relative is a Comté aged for twelve months.

STORAGE: Store for several weeks on the warmest shelf of the refrigerator, or in the crisper drawer wrapped in its original paper.

🍷 *Serve with dry white wine or a light red wine. Abondance is delicious with Savoie wine. A Ripaille AOC wine or a gamay will release its delicious aromas.*

"Many people don't like Abondance because of its slightly bitter flavor. But if you explain that the bitterness is a natural feature, like the bitterness of fine chocolate, any doubters will soon be won over to the cause!"

BANON AOC 2003

◆

**Soft cheese
Bloomy rind**

SEASON

SPRING SUMMER FALL WINTER

○ *Geography and Origin:* Banon cheese was born many years ago in the village of Banon, perched between Mont Ventoux and Mount Lure. It is said that in the second century the Roman Emperor Antonin Pius ate himself to death on it. In the Middle Ages, Banon resembled a Tome cheese and was wrapped in vine leaves. It was only later, when the vineyards developed phyloxera, that chestnut leaves were used. In addition to giving Banon its special flavor, the leaves protect the cheese from insects, thus lengthening its preservation. Less sticky than vine leaves, chestnut tree leaves became the norm in the nineteenth century. While Banon made from cow's milk once existed, today it has entirely disappeared and Banon is made exclusively with goat's milk, from the Provençal, Rove, or Alpine breeds.

○ *Choose the Best:* Banon is always presented in brown chestnut leaves, folded over and held in place with a length of raffia. Beneath the leaves the cheese has a cream-colored bloomy rind and a smooth, creamy interior. It should have a soft center and earthy aromas. The tannin of the chestnut leaves and the subtle flavor of the goat's cheese combine together deliciously and give Banon its unique character.

○ *How to Serve:* Serve with fruit bread and slices of Comice pear.

/ 🕮 / Its closest relatives are the Pélardon of Languedoc-Roussillon and the Picodon of the Rhône-Alpes region.

STORAGE: Refrigerate for only a few days wrapped in its chestnut leaves. Remove from the refrigerator at least thirty minutes before serving if you like it creamy with a pliable center. For people who like their cheeses more pungent and pronounced, it can be eaten dried.

🍷 *Banon requires a wine from the South. When it is pliable inside, taste it with a white Côtes-de-Provence. When drier, its stronger flavors pair well with some southeastern red wines, like Coteaux-d'Aix-en-Provence or a fuller bodied white wine like Saint-Joseph.*

"Its gown of chestnut leaves always stirs one's curiosity, and its Provençal origins always appeal. After all, who can say 'no' to Provence? All the beauty of the region is encapsulated in this small rounded disk of soft, bloomy rind cheese that genuinely blooms on the tongue!"

BEAUFORT AOC 1968

◆

Cooked
Pressed

SEASON

SPRING   SUMMER   FALL   WINTER

◦ *Geography and Origin:* Originating in the mid-to high mountains of eastern France, Beaufort already had a reputation as a fine cheese in Antiquity and the Middle Ages when it was traded for spices and textiles from Italy. Once known as "vachelin," it became known as Beaufort in 1865, although its production methods are still the same today. It is considered the jewel in the region's crown due to the richness of Alpine grazing land enjoyed by the cows.

◦ *Choose the Best:* The cheese is sold under three appellations: Beaufort, Beaufort d'été (summer Beaufort, produced from June to late October), and Beaufort Chalet d'Alpage. The latter is the most prestigious due to its strict AOP regulations: to achieve this appellation, the cheese has to be produced twice a day in alpine chalet conditions at an altitude of nearly five thousand feet, using the milk of a single herd while ensuring all *fermier* cheese criteria are met. Presented as a 14- to 30-inch wheel weighing between 55 and 150 pounds, Beaufort is recognizable from its concave heel. The color of its rind—from yellow to brown, according to its affinage—

should show no red pigmentation or black spots. During affinage it is smeared with morge, a controlled bacterial wash whose ingredients include whey or brine along with, possibly, wine or cheese scraps. Its rind is neither too dry nor too moist. After cutting, its ivory interior is never speckled and has a uniform color. It should have a smooth and clean texture, without holes or cracks, and it should never be rubbery or elastic. Its aromas, ranging from grassy and buttery to hazelnut, are balanced and varied without ever being overpowering. On the palate, the interior is firm then soft and pliable. It may feature a blue oval casein label that guarantees traceability (production workshop, day, and month of production); a red square casein label is used for Beaufort Chalet d'Alpage.

◦ *How to Serve:* An icon of Savoie cuisine, it is served as a fondue and as an accompaniment to a gratin of Savoyard buckwheat *crozet* pasta. It is never grated but instead finely sliced into shavings or cubes. Try a Beaufort soufflé or Beaufort gougères as an aperitif.

/ ☞ / Its closest relative is Comté.

STORAGE: Several weeks in the refrigerator in its original paper. Remove from the refrigerator 30 minutes before serving.

🍷 *A Savoie white wine such as an Apremont or a Roussette-de-Savoie, a Burgundy white, or Meursault—all are perfect with Beaufort. If it is young, you may also serve a light-bodied red wine. If aged, opt for the fruitier Roussette-de-Savoie or a full-bodied tannic red or fine white wine, like Hermitage or Corton.*

"At the risk of making myself unpopular, it is hard to find a good Beaufort. You have to trust your cheesemonger, because too many Beauforts are sold too young and are flavorless. My finest memory of a Beaufort was a wonderful wheel aged for eighteen months with a dark rind, the color of the Tarine and Abondance breed of cows."

BLEU D'AUVERGNE AOC 1975

◆

Blue cheese

SEASON

SPRING   SUMMER   FALL   WINTER

○ *Geography and Origin:* In 1845, a young Auvergnat, Antoine Roussel, decided to experiment by sprinkling his milk with some of the mold that had formed on his rye bread. In the process he invented blue cheese. He went on to perfect his method by piercing the cheese with needles to let the mold and air seep inside and develop. The cheese began to breathe and stabilize. The process was adopted by other Auvergnats, for other cheeses that are highly prized today. Only Ferrandaise and Salers cows can produce the milk for this blue cheese.

○ *Choose the Best:* Beneath the aluminum paper, the natural bloomy rind should be dry and not viscous with a white ivory interior, marbled with regular and uniform blue and green veins. The veins of mold blend with the salt impregnated in the interior and, on the palate, the blue tangy mold mingles magnificently with the interior's salty flavor. This blue cheese should be firm, not hard or fatty, to the touch. It has a pungent aroma full of its terroir, with notes of licorice, gentian, and anemone. On the palate, the interior is firm, creamy, and tender, not chalky or runny. Its texture is pliable and creamy, its flavor intense and full-bodied, but balanced with earthy, mushroom aromas.

○ *How to Serve:* Bleu d'Auvergne is a cheese of character, full of flavor and good for the digestion, so perfect for the end of the meal. It also works well as an aperitif, on canapés, and beaten into butter as a spread. Its flavor is enhanced with slices of pear and chunks of walnut. In salads it likes the bitter notes of endives and the sweetness of beet; it also works well crushed into vinaigrette. It brings an original note to soufflés, some meats, and as a seasoning for pasta dishes, quiches, and savory pancakes.

/ ☞ / Its closest relative is Fourme d'Ambert.

STORAGE: Two to three weeks in the refrigerator in its original aluminum paper, which helps it to mature and keeps it from drying out. Remove from the refrigerator at least an hour before consuming, especially if it is pre-sliced.

🍷 *Bleu d'Auvergne straight from the cave d'affinage loves white wines like Bergerac, Sauternes, a gewurztraminer, or even a Pineau-des-Charentes. The salty and earthy flavors of blue cheese combine well with a sweet white wine. Pair a maturing Bleu d'Auvergne with a Cabernet-d'Anjou and a more mature blue cheese with a full-bodied red wine.*

"Often considered to be the least flavorful of the French blues, perhaps because it is the least expensive, it is also the AOP cheese with the most interesting flavor-to-price ratio! A good Bleu d'Auvergne can be just as delectable as the rest of the blue family!"

BLEU DE GEX HAUT-JURA AOC 1977
OR BLEU DE SEPTMONCEL

◆

Blue cheese

SEASON

SPRING SUMMER FALL WINTER

○ *Geography and Origin:* The Gex region is found between the Jura Mountains and Lake Geneva. Its cheese was first produced and developed by the monks of the Abbey of Saint-Claude. It is possible that the production philosophy of Sassenage-style blue cheese was imported by migrants from the former province of Daphiné. In 1349, to repay his debts, their seigneur Humbert II gifted their land to the King of France. Refusing French rule, migrants from the province set off taking their cheese-making knowledge with them. In the sixteenth century, it was the favorite cheese of the regional ruler, Charles Quint. Today this delicious cheese, whose traditions of affinage have been passed on by word of mouth for generations, is now made solely with Montbeliard cow's milk within a delimited geographical zone with a very unique flora.

○ *Choose the Best:* The cheese is a smallish, plump, flat wheel with a rounded heel. It weighs between 13 to 20 pounds, and its size varies from 12 to 14 inches. Its rind is a yellowish white without mold. Its surface is smooth, dry, and slightly floury. Its interior has slight cracks and is ivory in color, marbled with uniformly distributed blue-green mold. Different to other blue cheeses, its interior is tender without being creamy and is slightly crumbly. Its aromas reveal light notes of mushroom and hazelnut. Slightly bitter with a salty edge, it is light yet flavorful, bringing all the wonders of the Haut-Jura to the palate.

○ *How to Serve:* Take a slice of Bleu de Gex and lay it on a thick slice of toasted country bread. Add several thin slices of dry-cured ham and broil until golden. You can also serve it with apples or pears.

/ 🖝 / Its closest relative is Fourme d'Ambert.

STORAGE: Two to three weeks in the refrigerator in its original aluminum paper, which helps it to mature and keeps it from drying out. Remove from the refrigerator at least an hour before consuming, especially if it is pre-sliced.

🍷 *A light, fruity red wine would be perfect. For a good local pairing, choose a Côtes-du-Jura or an Arbois vin de paille. For special occasions, try a Banyuls grand cru, which is a wonderful combination!*

"Bleu de Gex is a less well known cheese. It is seldom available in supermarkets and cheesemongers often do not promote it. At two months it is an absolute delight!"

BLEU
DES CAUSSES AOC 1991

◆

Blue cheese

SEASON

SPRING   SUMMER   FALL   WINTER

○ *Geography and Origin:* Born in Antiquity in the Midi-Pyrénées region, the specific, original qualities of Bleu des Causses comes from its *terroir* and its harsh, contrasting climate of moors and rocks. The flavor of the milk benefits from the aromas of the region's wild plants. The cheese is crafted by only a handful of dairies in the Causses region. There is no farmstead production and the cheese is matured in caves dug into the limestone scree slopes. The most humid part of the valley faces southeast, so the caves are riddled with fresh, damp breezes, encouraging the cheese's bloom, while giving it a gentle, yet intense flavor.

○ *Choose the Best:* Bleu des Causses is a regular or slightly deformed cylinder, with flat or slightly concave surfaces. The interior, with its even blue veins, is an ivory-yellow color, gleaming in summer, whiter and less humid in winter. The rind is clean, without excessive mold or spots. The interior consistency, at its best,

is creamy and smooth. It has a pronounced yet pleasant aroma of mushrooms (*Penicillium roqueforti*). It is a close relative of Roquefort in terms of production technique but has a very different flavor: on the palate, the texture is supple and pliable, with a pronounced flavor, sometimes tinged with a slight bitterness without being too tangy or too salty. It is a cheese of character, with a good blue-cheese aroma. Its flavor is more intense in winter.

○ *How to Serve:* Bleu des Causses served on fig bread is delicious at the end of the meal. Try it cooked in an omelet or in savory pancakes, as a seasoning for pasta or potatoes, or simply melted on a slice of bread broiled in the oven. You can also use it to thicken meat sauces—melting it into roast beef juices, for example—or you can serve it on broiled meat for a truly refined taste experience.

/ ☞ / Its closest relative is Roquefort.

STORAGE: The cheese can be stored for three weeks in the refrigerator, well wrapped in its original paper.

🍷 *Perfect with a powerful red, a Bordeaux, Cahors, or Madiran. If you want to tone down its character, try a natural sweet wine, or a fortified sweet wine like Maury or Rivesaltes.*

"More of an archetypal blue cheese than the other blues, especially Bleu d'Auvergne, it is also a little saltier, almost like a Roquefort. I'm surprised it has such a low profile."

BLEU
DU VERCORS-SASSENAGE AOC 1998

◆

Blue cheese

SEASON

SPRING   SUMMER   FALL   WINTER

○ *Geography and Origin:* Born in the Middle Ages in the Dauphinois region, Bleu du Vercors-Sassenage was long manufactured solely so that farmers could pay their farm duty to the seigneur of Sassenage, who was unable to collect their milk. It was only in 1338 that Baron Albert de Sassenage gave the inhabitants of Vercors the freedom to sell their cheeses. Since 2001, the cheese has its own festival staged in one of the villages of the Vercors natural park. Today it is made with cow's milk from the Montbeliard, Abondance, and Villard-de-Lans breeds.

○ *Choose the Best:* The cheese has perfectly flat surfaces and a curved convex heel. Its fine rind is smooth, dry, and uniform with a white and ivory-to-orange color, in equal proportion. The light yellow interior reveals the gentle even blue veins and there are regular fissures no longer than ⅓ inch. The gentle earthy blue cheese aromas also have hazelnut notes. On the palate, it is slightly salty and bitter. Its texture is pliable and even.

○ *How to Serve:* Serve with walnuts and white grapes. It can also be cooked and works well in leak or walnut pies or with pasta as a variation on spaghetti carbonara. Served with a simple leaf salad it is also perfect. For a true gourmet delight, toast it on bread and dip it in pumpkin soup.

/ ☞ / Its closest relative is Bleu de Laqueuille.

STORAGE: If protected in wax or parchment paper, it can keep for eight to fifteen days in the refrigerator. Remove from the refrigerator at least thirty minutes before serving, with or without its paper.

🍷 *A fresh and fruity, aromatic Côtes-du-Ventoux red will really bring out the full complexity of Bleu du Vercors-Sassenage. You can also try a Beaujolais or Côtes-du-Rhône.*

"It's a pity this cheese's reputation is not more widespread. Few cheesemongers outside the region offer this delectable blue cheese. It's an outrage! With its mushroom notes, it makes for an unforgettable blue cheese experience. I first discovered it when I entered the Meilleur Ouvrier de France competition."

BRIE DE MEAUX AOC 1980

◆

Soft cheese
Bloomy rind

SEASON

SPRING   SUMMER   FALL   WINTER

○ *Geography and Origin:* Since its creation, Brie de Meaux has never ceased to enchant the world. Once upon a time, it was farmers' daily fare and quite simply known as "Brie," indistinct from the other cheeses of the region, so bereft of the nobility that provenance brings. When it was finally dubbed "Brie de Meaux" and associated with Meaux, a distinguished provincial cathedral town with an Episcopal Palace, it developed commercial value. This Brie is an integral part of French history. It was present at the feast of Charlemagne's coronation in the year 800, then a thousand years later in 1815, it made an appearance at the Congress of Vienna where Talleyrand pronounced it the "king of cheeses." It is molded by hand with a special ladle, known as "pelle à brie"; in the past, cheesemongers presented it on wicker trays.

○ *Choose the Best:* Brie de Meaux has a bloomy rind with a light, velvety texture. When aged it might be scattered with red and brown pigments. The interior is supple and elastic, but with a certain firmness, and it has a creamy, light straw yellow color. This brie offers a generous array of flavors with distinct mushroom notes. On the palate, it should be creamy, with hints of hazelnut, and a long, pronounced, persistent flavor.

○ *How to Serve:* Brie de Meaux is great for cooking. In winter savor Brie de Meaux and pear tarts with a lamb's lettuce and walnut salad. It is also marvelous with fig or tomato preserve. Dried prunes really bring out its earthy flavors.

/ ☞ / Its closest relative is, above all, Camembert de Normandie (rather than Brie de Melun).

STORAGE: If ripe, store for twelve days at most in the refrigerator on the lowest shelf. Remove from the refrigerator an hour before serving to really express all its aromas. Store at room temperature if not entirely ripe.

🍷 *Try Brie de Meaux with a fruity, well-structured red from the Côte de Beaune region (Pommard, Volnay, Monthélie, Saint-Aubin, . . .), which will offer interesting notes. If the cheese isn't quite ripe, opt for a more mineral white wine—an Anjou or Vouvray, for example, would make perfect partners!*

"It is without doubt one of the best-known cheeses. When it is ripe, tender, and creamy, with its rich aromas of mushroom and fresh cow's milk, it is always a big hit. A ripe Brie de Meaux is quite simply mouthwatering. Often guests will sit and gaze at it, not daring to disturb its beauty."

BRIE
DE MELUN AOC 1980

◆

**Soft cheese
Bloomy rind**

SEASON

SPRING · SUMMER · FALL · WINTER

○ *Geography and Origin:* History tells us that Brie de Melun was already a big favorite with France's early medieval royalty: Charlemagne, Robert II, and Philip II included. The famous French fabulist, Jean de La Fontaine, turned it into the star of his famous fable, *The Crow and the Fox*, before Talleyrand took it to the Congress of Vienna with its neighbor, Brie de Meaux, to show off the wonders of France (an occasion when its neighbor from Brie unfortunately stole the show, see previous pages). Since 1995, the fellowship, Chevaliers du Brie de Melun, has campaigned passionately for its preservation and promotion of the cheese that is said to be the "ancestor of all bries."

○ *Choose the Best:* Like its relative from Meaux, it is a flat wheel, but Brie de Melun is smaller. Its fine, slightly crinkled rind speckled with red pigments may sometimes seem sticky and have brown specks. The dominant aromas are creamy and earthy, with notes of mushroom, leather, and damp earth. On the palate, Brie de Melun gives a powerful, distinctive, almost musky flavor that is delicious. It should be eaten when its interior is mostly creamy and ripe to the center.

○ *How to Serve:* Add this Brie to a quiche lorraine, for example—the combination is exquisite. The most simple and effective: when completely ripe, eat it with a fine white country bread.

/ ☞ / Its closest relative is Brie de Meaux.

STORAGE: It can be kept for about ten days in its original wrapping paper, but never in plastic wrap or in aluminum paper. It is best stored on a wooden board beneath a glass cheese dome. Store in the coldest part of the refrigerator. Warning: If it dries out, it loses all its flavor.

🍷 *Like its close relative, Brie de Meaux, accompany this cheese with a robust but elegant Burgundy wine, like a Gevrey-Chambertin. Côtes-du-Rhône or Saumur-Champigny, also works well. For special occasions, try a Saint-Nicolas-de-Bourgueil: it is a robust pairing but a real joy.*

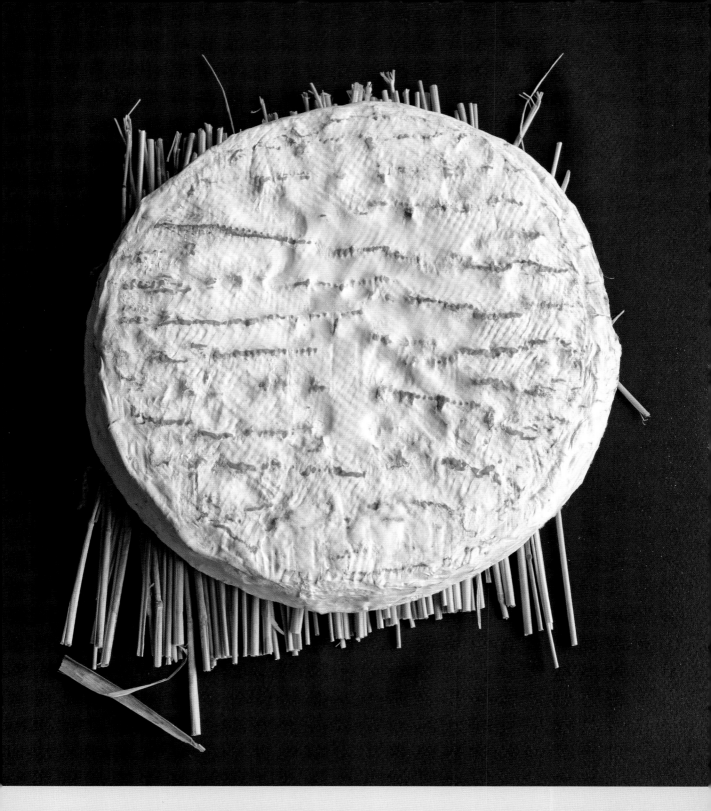

"Brie de Melun has a lower profile than its relative from Meaux, which is surprising given its creamy complexity. It is smaller than Brie de Meaux and at the same age expresses greater flavor. When perfectly ripe, newcomers are instantly seduced. Tasting is believing!"

BROCCIU
OR BROCCIU CORSE ^{AOC 1983}

◆

**Fresh
cheese**

SEASON

SPRING   SUMMER   FALL   WINTER

○ *Geography and Origin:* According to legend, a cruel ogre living in a dolmen, known locally as Casa di l'Urcu, used to terrorize neighboring goatherds, stealing their ewes and goats. The furious goatherds decided to kill the monster. They captured the ogre but the ogre held the secret of Brocciu (pronounced "brotch-i-oo"), and promised to share the secret in exchange for his freedom. The shepherds agreed to the deal, demanding he surrender the recipe before release. The ogre surrendered his secret but the goatherds still killed him. Today an emblematic product of Corsica, Brocciu is produced from whey, drained from the whole milk of the Corsican goat or the Corsican and Sardinian ewe. The whey is then heated and then salted to produce a flaky, milky mousse, which is then skimmed into small pots, similar to *faisselles*; artisanal production uses small rush baskets called *canestres*.

○ *Choose the Best:* Brocciu should weigh between ½ pound and 7 pounds. It can be served fresh or *passu*,

i.e. saltier and more mature. When fresh, its color ranges from immaculate white to cream, while its texture is firm and creamy on the palate, with a light, pleasant, slightly salty flavor. The fresher it is, the tenderer and smoother it is. When mature, or *passu*, its color is darker and its texture firmer, with a downy rind and a more pronounced flavor. It is sold as *fermier*, artisanal or dairy, in small pots (like *faisselles*) on which you will see the label "brocciu frais."

○ *How to Serve:* Brocciu is delicious hot and cold. It is an integral part of Corsican cookery and is found in the traditional *fiadone*, a kind of Brocciu cheese flan, with eggs, sugar, a sprinkling of flour, and lemon zest. When cooked, it works amazingly as a stuffing for filo pastry parcels or raviolis, and, like other goat's and ewe's cheeses, it combines deliciously with spinach and pine nuts, for example. It turns an omelet into a gourmet delight. Try serving fresh Brocciu as a dessert with chestnut liqueur or simply sprinkle it with brown sugar.

/ ☞ / Its closest relative is Greuil du Béarn.

STORAGE: Brocciu keeps for several days in the refrigerator when fresh and several weeks when mature.

🍷 *It combines well with Corsican wines. Fresh Brocciu can be served with a gentle and sweet Muscat-du-Cap-Corse, or any other muscat grape variety wines. For Brocciu* passu, *opt for a more structured wine: Ajaccio or Côtes-de-Provence. For dry Brocciu, go for a more robust Patrimonio, Fitou, or Corbières, etc.*

"Often wrongly confused with non-beaten white cheese, the texture of which doesn't appeal to children, this fresh cheese, produced from heated ewe's or goat's whey, has even more flavor than its close relative, Brousse."

CAMEMBERT DE NORMANDIE AOC 1983

◆

**Soft cheese
Bloomy rind**

SEASON

SPRING   SUMMER   FALL   WINTER

○ *Geography and Origin:* Local legend has it that it was the humble cheesemaker, Marie Harel, who invented the cheese in the village of Camembert in the eighteenth century. What is for certain is that it was the cheesemaking dynasty she initiated that began the great Camembert adventure. In 1863, a descendant of Harel's introduced Emperor Napoleon III to his mother's pride and joy when he visited the region. The Emperor was so impressed that Paris's restaurants instantly adopted "Napoleon III's cheese" on their menus. From 1880, it became readily transportable when engineer Eugène Ridel created a small wooden box in which to keep it. Until this point the cheese was generally covered in a wild blue velvety rind over which producers had no control, but in 1910, it suddenly turned white when, in a flash of foodie inspiration, producers decided to spray it with *Penicillium candidum*.

○ *Choose the Best:* This small wheel with its straight heel, angular edges and parallel undulating sides, has a thin, white, bloomy rind, with a downy complexion showing occasional signs of red pigmentation. The middle of the creamy yellow interior sometimes develops small fermentation bubbles. It has a certain suppleness to it: when pressed it should return to its former shape. It is a solid cheese that is not runny. The layering of its unripe center reveals its original molding. On the palate, the texture should be neither too pliable nor too sticky. It has a pronounced well-balanced, slightly salty flavor. Camembert de Normandie should not have a neutral flavor, nor be too tart, bitter, or excessively or insufficiently salty. Delicately intense and persistent, its aromas are lactic (butter and cream), fruity, with sulfuric hints of garlic and cabbage, as well as an earthy fragrance with hints of mushroom. To appreciate its full complexity of aromas, you should choose a Camembert de Normandie marked "au lait cru, moulé à la louche," i.e raw milk, ladle-molded.

○ *How to Serve:* Bake in flaky pastry, as a gratin, or in a terrine. Try a Camembert tart, covered in slices of pear, apricot, or apple, for that regional touch.

/ ☞ / Its closest relative is Brie de Meaux.

STORAGE: Ten or so days in its original packaging. If mature, keep refrigerated and remove an hour before serving. If it is not matured to the center, store at room temperature.

🍷 *The ideal pairing is farmstead cider, especially for a nice, ripe Camembert!*

"My grandmother used to say that Camembert 'stinks of the devil,' and she would set it aside on her display shelves. She was also baffled by why so many people bought it, but without realizing she had paid the greatest possible tribute to a cheese by showcasing it alone, hence piquing the curiosity of all."

CANTAL ^{AOC 1956}

◆

Uncooked pressed cheese

SEASON

SPRING   SUMMER   FALL   WINTER

○ *Geography and Origin:* Cantal takes its name from the mountain range it comes from. In the first century AD, Pliny the Elder mentioned it in his *Natural History* as the most popular cheese in Rome. Throughout its history, various writings have mentioned it as "*formes*" or "*fourmes de Cantal.*" It is undisputably one of Europe's oldest cheeses.

○ *Choose the Best:* After only thirty days ripening, the rind of a young, or *jeune*, Cantal is white and its interior is light colored with a very pronounced milk flavor. The more time passes, the more its rind becomes spotted, revealing red-orange pigments. Its interior then turns white and changes texture. Its flavor is persistent with aromas of butter and cream and hints of greenery such as gentian. After ripening for two to six months, Cantal is called entre-deux. The cheese's flavor expresses all the robustness of its *terroir*: there are pronounced aromas of hazelnut, spices, and pepper with animal notes. Its interior may become slightly crumbly. After six months of ripening, Cantal is called vieux Cantal and is full of character. Some Cantal is matured in former railway tunnels and this, some say, is when it is at its best!

○ *How to Serve:* Serve Cantal cold or hot at any point of the meal. Diced as an aperitif, grated into soup (sprinkle onto onion soup, for example, then place beneath the broiler), or beat into creamy mashed potatoes. On a platter, try serving it at all three stages of its maturity: *jeune*, *entre-deux*, and *vieux*, with dried fruits.

/ ☞ / Young Cantal's closest relative is Cheddar; a Laguiole aged for five months is closest to Cantal *entre-deux*; and Salers most resembles Cantal *vieux*.

STORAGE: Fifteen days in good-quality waxed paper on the coldest shelf of the refrigerator so as not to disturb its flavor. Remove from the refrigerator at least an hour before serving.

🍷 *The age of the cheese determines the pairing. For a young Cantal opt for a Saumur-Champigny or white Graves; an* entre-deux *or* vieux *Cantal would prefer a Haut-Médoc, the perfect pairing. Other spicy, tannic red wines would also work with a Cantal vieux: Saint-Chinian, Corbières, Pauillac, etc.*

"At home we call it 'table cheese,' possibly because for so long it was one of the least expensive cheeses on the market, making it a common feature of daily household life."

CHABICHOU DU POITOU

AOC 1990

◆

**Soft cheese
Natural rind**

SEASON

| SPRING | SUMMER | FALL | WINTER |

○ *Geography and Origin:* According to legend, Chabichou appeared in the eighth century after the defeat of Arab troops by Charles Martel in Poitiers. When Umayyad forces retreated back to Iberia in 732, following the Battle of Tours, among the belongings they left behind were their goats; the word "chabichou" comes from the word *cheblis,* meaning "goat" in Arabic. Locals soon caught onto the idea of making cheese with the newfound animals' milk and Chabichou was born. In the sixteenth century, the author Rabelais, known for his epicurean tastes and love of good food, dubbed it the "best cheese in France." And with very good reason: the Chabichou du Poitou encapsulates all the floral richness and wonder of the Haut-Poitou and its limestone plateaus, which include a variety of different grasses, red clover, alfalfa, and legumes. The cheese is made solely with milk from the Alpine, Saanen, and Poitevine breeds.

○ *Choose the Best:* The Chabichou du Poitou is similar to its neighbor the Bonde de Gâtine. It has a fine white rind, the same color as its firm, supple interior. It may be *jeune* (between fresh and two weeks of maturation), *demi-sec* (four weeks of *affinage*) or sec or *affiné* (six weeks of *affinage*), or very dry (eight weeks of *affinage*). When young, it has a subtle goaty aroma and a smooth, even, non-creamy interior. With a few weeks' maturation, it becomes harder and its rind develops red spots. As it ages, its interior becomes drier and crumblier, with a more pronounced, sharper flavor, like its odor. Depending on its *affinage,* Chabichou du Poitou has musty, earthy aromas with notes of mushroom, cut grass, ripe fruits, hazelnuts, and even cocoa and toasted almonds. A full meal in itself!

○ *How to Serve:* In summer, try stuffing ripe tomatoes with Chabichou du Poitou instead of meat: the result is wondrous! You can also cook fillets of sole with Chabichou sauce, or serve it on toast or in cubes as an aperitif with a sweet Pineau-des-Charentes.

/ ☞ / Its closest relative is Pouligny-Saint-Pierre.

STORAGE: Fifteen days in the crisper drawer or three weeks if it is dry. Remove from the refrigerator an hour before eating.

🍷 *A sauvignon is the ideal partner, but a chardonnay is also a good choice. Lighter, gentler wines are ideal, especially dry white wines.*

"I have such fond memories of this cheese from my vacation on Île de Ré. It is lesser known than other cheeses from central France but offers the best that goat's cheese has to bring. It is so good that I have always tended to eat it unaccompanied, without bread, even."

CHAOURCE AOC 1970

◆

Soft cheese
Bloomy rind

SEASON

SPRING   SUMMER   FALL   WINTER

○ *Geography and Origin:* While its name comes from the town of Chaource, this cheese is so old its origins are uncertain. It is said that Cistercian monks from Pontigny—responsible for planting the vineyards of Chablis—created this cheese. There are insufficient existing written sources to pinpoint its history with any accuracy. It is known that the farmers of Chaource once offered their overlord, the Bishop of Langres, "111 capons and 136 cheeses"; the Bishop is renowned in French history for his gargantuan appetite. In the fourth century, King Charles IV le Bel enjoyed its delights when visiting the region and it is said that Margeret of Burgundy, Queen of Sicily, always demanded it be served at meal times, as she insisted on always keeping the finest company. Today it is made with cow's milk from brown Alpine and Frisonne breeds.

○ *Choose the Best:* Chaource is a small, plump regular wheel. It has a slightly pitted, downy white rind without mold. The interior is white, pliable and even. Chaource ripens from the outside-in, from the creamy rind to its chalky center. It has aromas of milk, cream, and fresh mushroom. When perfectly ripe, it expresses aromas of hazelnut, cream, milk, and mushroom. It comes in two sizes: large (1 pound) or small (½ pound). In the past it was wrapped in straw or dried plane tree leaves and placed in sandstone pitchers to ripen. Today it is matured on wicker trays.

○ *How to Serve:* Serve with a mixed leaf salad and a strong, mustardy vinaigrette or spread on a hot crusty baguette. For a special regional flavor, serve it with whole-grain Dijon mustard.

/ ☞ / Its closest relative is Brillat-Savarin.

STORAGE: Eight to ten days, ideally beneath a glass cheese dome. Today, people are fond of storing it with a stick of cinnamon.

🍷 *With a young Chaource, serve a Chablis, Coteaux-Champenois, or a pinot-gris from Alsace. For a mature Chaource, opt for a robust Burgundy red, like Irancy, Nuits-Saint-Georges, or a Pommard. You could also try Chaource with champagne, even if, at first, it does seem a daring pairing.*

"I first tasted this cheese in quite exceptional circumstances, accompanied with a fine rosé Champagne. Conserved beneath a glass cheese dome to protect it from the air, it will ripen on its own accord. If you move the glass cheese dome, delicious mushroomy aromas escape."

CHAROLAIS AOC 2010

AOC 2010

◆

**Soft cheesee
Natural rind**

SEASON

SPRING   SUMMER   FALL   WINTER

○ *Geography and Origin:* The history of Charolais cheese dates back to the sixteenth century when farmers on the hills of Charolais, in Burgundy, decided to raise goats as well as their eponymous cattle. It should be recalled that the goat was long considered to be the "poor man's cow." Surrounded by bountiful prairies and woodland, Charolais farmers produced good yields of goat's milk and soon began to make cheese, which they named after their region. Known as a *fromage de ménage*, a household cheese, in the past workers would buy fresh Charolais and let it mature in small cages known as "chazières" or "tsézires" until dry. Charolais is one of the most developed goat's milk cheeses made from milk from the Alpine and Saanen goats.

○ *Choose the Best:* Resembling a small barrel, Charolais has a dense and smooth white interior. After two weeks *affinage*, it takes on the aromas of plants, grasses, hay, and fresh straw. When more mature, pronounced earthy, buttery, and mushroom notes appear and its texture becomes drier and more brittle.

○ *How to Serve:* A cake with dry-cured ham, pears, and Charolais cut into chunks—perfect with a younger Charolais. Try broiling it in slices with herbs sprinkled on top. It is also delicious with fig and walnut preserve.

/ ☞ / Its closest relative is Tour du Montot, an exceptional cheese.

STORAGE: It can be stored eight to fifteen days in its waxed paper on a plate in a cool closet, if not yet matured (its dense interior will crack in the refrigerator). If already dry, store in the refrigerator and remove one hour before serving to appreciate its full flavors all the way through to the middle.

🍷 *Born amid the vineyards, Charolais pairs perfectly with the gourmet delights of its* terroir: *try a white Rully, a Mâcon-Villages, or a Chablis, which work magnificently with this cheese and its round aromas. If you are fond of fruity red wines made with pinot noir, cabernet franc, or gamay—like a Beaujolais, Touraine, or Anjou—then pair it with a more mature Charolais.*

"Charolais has a special place in my heart. I love this Burgundy cheese: it is full of aromas and its special shape makes it instantly visible in our displays. I especially love it when the cheese is covered in blue mold concealing 3 to 4 mm [.11 to .15 inch] of cream."

CHAVIGNOL
OR CROTTIN DE CHAVIGNOL ^{AOC 1976}

◆

**Soft cheese
Natural rind**

SEASON

SPRING   SUMMER   FALL   WINTER

○ *Geography and Origin:* Chavignol comes from the small village of Chavignol in the Berry region. Its origins are difficult to trace. The word "crottin" probably comes from the word "crot" meaning "hole" in local Berry dialect—crots were watering holes where women would wash linen. From the clay around the crots, people made oil lamps and these lamps were used to mold and drain the goat curd. In 1829, a census of the Cher department states that "cheeses from the Sancerrois goat are known as 'Crottin de Chavignolles.'" In 2017 it was decreed that Crottin de Chavignol could only be made with milk from the Alpine breed.

○ *How to choose the best?* Crottin de Chavignol comes in several forms—choose it young, blue, or mature (*frais, demi-sec,* or *sec*). The more mature it is, the stronger the character. When young, its white interior is appreciated for its gentle, sweet freshness. Blue, it is creamy and suave. Very dry, it has a powerful flavor without any bitterness. It is a small, flat, slightly plump disk, adopting the form of its truncated molds. Its fine rind may have white or blue mold. The interior is white to ivory, even, smooth, and firm, sometimes brittle if very mature. It has a rich goat's milk flavor. When the cheese is dry, some locals finish maturing it in eau-de-vie or wine. Such cheeses are a rarity and generally only found locally. The taste is surprising but well worth trying.

○ *How to Serve:* When fresh, cover it in breadcrumbs and serve with young leaf salad drizzled with olive oil and duck prosciutto. When dry, try it in a salad of well-seasoned arugula.

/ ☞ / Its closest relative is Chabichou du Poitou.

STORAGE: Eight to fifteen days at room temperature in a cool closet or refrigerator, marinated in a pot of olive oil with herbs and aromatics.

🍷 *A fresh Crottin works well with a white Sancerre. An aged Crottin works better with red Sancerre. Opt for red wines that are not too tannic, or a dry white.*

"I'm very fond of Crottin de Chavignol. It is too often copied with generic goat's cheese *crottins* available every-where. The true Crottin de Chavignol is inimitable. In restaurants, make sure that the Crottin you order is indeed 'de Chavignol.' When dry, it is an unforgettable gourmet experience."

CHEVROTIN AOC 2002

◆

Uncooked pressed

SEASON

SPRING SUMMER FALL WINTER

○ *Geography and Origin:* An exclusively *fermier* production with raw milk, since the seventeenth century Chevrotin has been hand-made using a unique method for goat's cheese production. Like Reblochon, it is an uncooked pressed cheese with a washed rind. It is always aged on spruce trays and turned at least three times per week. It is produced in the heart of the steepest, sheerest mountain slopes, where only the Alpine breed of goat is capable of grazing the rich and diverse vegetation growing on the limestone foothills of the northern Alps.

○ *Choose the Best:* This small wheel weighs approximately 10½ ounces and looks like a small Reblochon. Its interior is soft and creamy. When ripe, its rind has a pink hue and on the palate, it gives a gentle flavor of goat's milk, with floral and lactic notes.

○ *How to Serve:* Bake Chevrotin in the oven with wild garlic: rub a small ramekin with garlic then add half a Chevrotin and bake in the oven until the cheese has melted.

/ 🖝 / Its closest relative is the Petit Fiancé des Pyrénées.

STORAGE: Eight to ten days on its spruce tray in its original wrapping paper, as for Reblochon. If matured, store in the refrigerator and remove one hour before serving to bring it to room temperature.

🍷 *Chevrotin likes robust, structured wines whether white or red. Opt for a dry white, preferably of the roussanne grape variety, common in the Savoie region. You can also try a mondeuse or Chignin-Bergeron from Savoie, a Saint-Joseph, or a Côte-Rôtie from the Rhône region or a Bandol for reds. Make sure the red is well aged and that the tannins have softened so as not to disturb the fruity aromas of the Chevrotin.*

"Another underestimated cheese that is too often overlooked on cheese platters. Perhaps because of the region's fine and famous cow's milk cheeses of the region constantly upstaging it. The Chevrotin makes for a delectable surprise off the beaten track!"

COMTÉ ^{AOC 1958}

AOC 1958

◆

Cooked
pressed

SEASON

SPRING SUMMER FALL WINTER

○ *Geography and Origin:* Created in the thirteenth century, *fruitieries* are crucial to Comté production and are what makes it unique. Living in small, isolated, tight-knit mountain communities, farmers pooled their resources by taking their milk to the *fructerie*, as it was then called, enabling them to make cheeses of a larger size that could be kept for longer—the perfect solution for surviving the long harsh winters ahead. Today, Comté is produced as a huge wheel of cheese—21 to 30 inches in diameter, weighing up to 100 pounds, and requiring roughly 120 gallons of cow's milk from Montbeliard and Simmental cows. In the sixteenth century, farmers transported Comté to Lyon to sell it. Around 1880, it became known as "gruyère de comté," and around 1950, simply as "Comté."

○ *Choose the Best:* On the heel you will find a green label, which means the cheese has been awarded a grade of 14 out of 20 by the AOP syndicate, or if the label is brown, the cheese has been graded 12-14. Flavor is not the only criterion: a brown label Comté can be good but its interior may present certain flaws. Cheeses with a grade below twelve are not allowed to bear the "Comté" appellation. The rind is granular, with yellow to brown coloring; the interior is firm, ivory to yellow, depending on the time of year. The interior is yellower in summer because the cows eat carotene-rich grass; it is more ivory in winter because the cows are fed on lower-carotene hay. But this does not mean that winter cheeses are inferior to summer Comtés. Depending on affinage, from four to fourteen months, Comté is often characterized doux or *fruité* ("gentle" or "fruity."). When aged, the flavors are more varied and pronounced with notes of hazelnut and floral and/or lactic nuances. There are six types of flavor that emerge: lactic, fruit, roasted, plant, animal, and spiced notes. Before buying a Comté, ask your cheesemonger if you can taste it.

○ *How to Serve:* In a gratin or dip sticks of Comté into soft-boiled egg. When Comté is aged, you can let it melt on your tongue like fine chocolate.

/ ☞ / Its closest relative is Beaufort.

STORAGE: Comté can be stored for a long time in the refrigerator in its original wrapping paper or in waxed paper, so as not to let the interior dry out.

🍷 *Comté is perfect with a* vin jaune *from the Jura with its intense notes of walnut and toasted almonds. Vin jaune is a very particular white wine, which is consumed at room temperature; it is the ideal choice with Comté and really lets its flavors emerge. Otherwise, a gentle, round Pomerol red is also delightful.*

"Comté is the most consumed cheese in France and has a huge reputation. Don't be afraid to ask your cheese-monger about the origin of the cheese in relation to the *fruitière* it comes from, the season it was produced, and its age and affinage temperatures to find the right Comté for you."

ÉPOISSES AOC 1991

◆

**Soft cheese
Washed rind**

SEASON

SPRING   SUMMER   FALL   WINTER

○ *Geography and Origin:* Epoisses dates back to the sixteenth century, when Cistercian monks started letting cheeses mature for several weeks and washed them in a mixture of brine and Marc de Bourgogne, a pomace brandy distilled from Burgundy wine. The recipe was passed along to farms in the region and the techniques were passed on from mother to daughter, all the while improving the method. Epoisses was featured at the dinner table in Louis XIV's court and was proclaimed the "king of all cheeses" by Brillat-Savarin in the nineteenth century, when it met with real commercial success. It nearly disappeared between the two world wars, but today it has rediscovered its full luster and is one of the most popular cheeses in France. It is made from cow's milk from the Brune, Montbeliard, and Simmental breeds.

○ *Choose the Best:* Epoisses exists in both small and large formats, in 9- to 12-ounce boxes or in 1½ pound- to 2½-pound wheels, sold by weight. The color of its rind varies from ivory orange to brick red due to the development of the *Brevibacterium linens*. Its rind is soft, slightly wrinkled, and glossy. The interior is supple, slightly resistant to the knife, creamy, and light beige in color. The center develops its smooth creamy texture as it matures. It has a fruity aroma with earthy, mushroom, slightly animal notes with a scent of the stable. It is often said that it offers the true smell of the countryside. Slightly salty on the palate, its flavor matches its aromas.

○ *How to Serve:* Serve on hot potatoes but also on a gratin dauphinois to really enhance the flavor. At the end of a meal, it is often the star of the cheese platter. It is best appreciated simply spooned from the plate.

/ 🖙 / Its closest relatives are its local rivals Ami du Chambertin and Trou du Cru.

STORAGE: Eight to ten days in the box in the warmest part of the refrigerator, which replicates the ideal affinage conditions. Remove from the refrigerator an hour before serving to awaken the aromas.

🍷 *After four weeks of affinage, Epoisses is perfect with an aged white Burgundy (Chassagne-Montrachet, Meursault) or an Alsace Pinot Gris Vendanges Tardives. With a more mature Epoisses, try a Gevrey-Chambertin or a Savigny-lès-Beaune. Pairing with red wine, however, is always risky.*

"Some claim that Epoisses is France's finest cheese. I am a big fan, not only for its flavor, but for everything it represents. It has a charm that appeals to the newbie as well as all the finesse and flavor to appeal to the seasoned cheese lover in search of balance and intensity."

LA FOURME D'AMBERT AOC 1972

♦

Blue cheese

SEASON

SPRING SUMMER FALL WINTER

○ *Geography and Origin:* The history of this cheese dates back to at least the eighth century. In feudal times in the Forez region, Fourme d'Ambert was made at temporary farms set up during the summer grazing season in shacks, known as *jasseries*, which were used as both stables and habitation. Along with eggs, dried sausage, butter, ham, and hay, farmers used the cheese to pay their tithes. A likeness of the cheese can be found sculpted above the entrance to a medieval chapel in La Chaume, which overlooks the region. It is also possible the cheese existed before the Middle Ages and, according to legend, Gaulish druids were particularly fond of it. The name *Fourme* comes from the same Latin root, "forma" as *fromage*, the French word for cheese, meaning "form."

○ *Choose the Best:* Fourme d'Ambert is either artisanal or dairy; there is no *fermier* Fourme. Its dry, slightly bloomy rind is a pearl gray color. Beneath is a supple, creamy interior with dense, uniform blue veins of *Penicillium glaucum*, which make this particular blue cheese gentler than others. To the nose there is a gentle musty cellar aroma. To identify a ripe Fourme, in local cheesemaking jargon, the cheese has to "make like an elephant's foot": the *affineur* turns the truckle upright and if it sags downward as though about to buckle, it bears a passing resemblance to an elephant's foot. And when this effect is achieved, the cheese is ready.

○ *How to Serve:* Serve Fourme d'Ambert throughout the meal. Its sweetish flavor makes it a perfect accompaniment for savory and sweet dishes. It works well with hazelnuts and walnuts, pears and apples. It suits a variety of breads.

/ ☞ / Its closest relatives are Bleu d'Auvergne and Bleu de Gex Haut-Jura.

STORAGE: Several days in the refrigerator in its original wrapping paper. If young, it can be stored for several weeks. Remove from the refrigerator an hour before serving to release its full aromas.

🍷 *A classic pairing would be a light, fruity red Côte-Roannaise, or a red gamay. For a more daring pairing, try Maury, a fortified sweet wine, which offers an interesting contrast with the blue flavors of the Fourme d'Ambert. Instead of Maury, you could try a Banyuls, a Rivesaltes* tuilé, *or a Porto.*

"Fourme is instantly recognizable by its towering barrel shape, or truckle. Many refuse to eat the top edges, because the look of such a dense blue rind can be off-putting. But it is here at the rind, which separates the rich center of the cheese from the outside world, that the most interesting aromas occur."

FOURME DE MONTBRISON ^{AOC 1972}

◆

Blue cheese

SEASON

SPRING   SUMMER   FALL   WINTER

○ *Geography and Origin:* Fourme de Montbrison dates back to ancient times. It was probably already produced by early Arverne tribes in the seventh to second centuries BC, long before the Roman conquest. It is said that Julius Caesar enjoyed a meal of Fourme de Montbrison as he forged his way across the Forez Mountains to attack the Gaulish warriors. Fourme de Montbrison and Fourme d'Ambert were long believed to be the same cheese, but they have their own distinctive characters, even though their separate AOP status was only accorded in 2002. In terms of production, their draining and salting techniques are different: Fourme de Montbrison is salted more during the curd-molding stage.

○ *Choose the Best:* Fourme de Montbrison is another tall cylindrical barrel roughly five inches in diameter. Its cream color is lighter and it has fewer blue veins than its neighbor from Ambert; its rind is an orange-red. Its texture is crumbly and its flavor ranges from fruity to robust, depending on maturity.

○ *How to Serve:* This Fourme melts beautifully so is marvelous in a variety of dishes, especially in gratins. Lay slices on mushroom soup and place beneath the broiler. For a regional pairing, slice onto fried eggs then place beneath the broiler.

/ ☞ / Its closest French-cheese relative is Fourme d'Ambert. From a taste perspective, it greatly resembles the English raw milk blue cheese Stichelton.

STORAGE: Several days in the refrigerator in its original wrapping paper. If young, it can be stored for several weeks. Remove from the refrigerator an hour before serving to release its full aromas.

🍷 *Fourme de Montbrison is a gentler, sweeter cheese so avoid wines that are too robust. Select a supple light, round companion, like a Grand Roussillon rosé, a Rivesaltes tuilé, a Banyuls grand cru, or a Jurançon Vendanges Tardives.*

"Too few cheese lovers know this cheese. It is often compared to the Fourme d'Ambert but is very different. Its drier interior and aromas of walnuts and forest mushrooms will delight you."

LAGUIOLE ^{AOC 1961}

◆

 | Uncooked pressed cheese | |

SEASON

SPRING   SUMMER   FALL   WINTER

○ *Geography and Origin:* Laguiole is one of France's oldest cheeses, thought to date from the fourth century. Manuscripts from the time and, later, Pliny the Elder described cheeses from the Aubrac region that are very similar to the Laguiole of today, though the cheese wasn't specifically mentioned by name in these writings. In the twelfth century, the monks of the Domerie d'Aubrac monastery determined its terroir using milk from Aubrac and Simmental cows that grazed on rich mountain pasture despite the harsh climate. They also elaborated its distinctive production process, which has been passed down through the generations and which creates a cheese with an extraordinary capacity for storage.

It has had its moments of glory, especially in the nineteenth century, but it nearly disappeared in the early twentieth century as industrialization drew the rural workforce to the city.

○ *Choose the Best:* Laguiole rind has attractive amber brown spots, which seem as if they are sewn to its thick skin. At its best, these spots proliferate and can be felt to the touch. Its interior should not be brittle, crumbly, soft, or too hard, but it should be firm and supple. Its color is even with a slightly marbled effect. Stray blue veins inside are a flaw. It has lactic aromas but should not smell like whey or ammonia. Like its calm, tranquil exterior, Laguiole should be balanced—neither too salty, nor too acid and bitter. Its texture should be pliable. Its aromas linger in the mouth, especially its delicious hazelnut notes.

○ *How to Serve:* Serve as a sauce for fish or sprinkle onto onion soup and place under the broiler. You could also serve it cubed as an aperitif with a glass of champagne, as a snack, or at the end of the meal with crusty country bread. Laguiole is perfect for cooking and makes a wonderful replacement for grated cheese on any gratin. It is also marvelous in burgers. Children love it!

/ ☞ / Its closest relatives are Cantal *entre-deux* or Salers aged six months.

STORAGE: Stores for two weeks in the refrigerator in its original wrapping paper. Remove from the refrigerator an hour before serving to release its full aromas.

🍷 *For a regional touch, choose a fruity wine from southern France, such as Cahors. It will also be delicious with gewurztraminer. For a young cheese, opt for a lighter wine, such as Gaillac, Limoux, or Bergerac. Older Laguiole prefers more robust wines such as Marcillac.*

"Laguiole is so very similar to Cantal but so very different. The difference lies in the all-important terroir: its climate differs from the Auvergne, bathing in the southern warmth of the Midi-Pyrénées. To cheese lovers it is instantly recognizable: their favorite is a Laguiole aged twelve months."

LANGRES ^{AOC 1991}

♦

Soft cheese
Washed rind

SEASON

SPRING SUMMER FALL WINTER

○ *Geography and Origin:* Langres dates back to medieval or even Roman times, like the town from which it originates. The first written trace of the cheese is in a song written by the Dominican prior of Langres. Like many other cheeses of the period, for many centuries Langres was a *fromage de ménage*, a household cheese, created for farming folks' personal consumption, and molded in stoneware containers. The cheese was then dried and matured on the leaves of plane trees, then on oat straw. Today, Langres is still made with cow's milk from the Montbeliard, Simmental, and Brune breeds.

○ *Choose the Best:* Langres is cylindrical with a hollow at the top known as the "fountain," which connoisseurs fill with the local pomace brandy, Marc de Bourgogne. The hollower the "fountain," the more mature the cheese. When this hollow exists, it is because the cheese is seldom turned during maturation. There are three formats, large (1¾ to 3 pounds), medium (10 to 12 ounces) and small (5¼ to 9 ounces). Its rind varies from light yellow to darker orange, depending on its maturity. Within its fine, wrinkled rind is a white to light beige interior, which can become darker over time. It is often creamy and it has a powerful, penetrating, and sometimes persistent aroma that leaves nobody indifferent. Its closest rival is its regional neighbor, Epoisses.

○ *How to Serve:* Prick the fountain with a fork, add a tablespoon of white wine, champagne, or whatever you feel like, then leave it beneath a glass cheese dome for twelve hours, so the cheese can absorb the wine. Another possibility, and a definite showstopper: flambé the cheese with Marc de Champagne. For this, choose a slightly drier Langres and place it in the oven. As soon as the rind becomes runny, remove it from the oven and flambé the cheese. A truly delicious taste experience!

/ ☞ / Its closest relative is a Belgian cheese, Remoudou.

STORAGE: Eight to twelve days in the refrigerator in its original packaging. Never store it hollow-down. You can also age it beneath a glass cheese dome, especially if you fill the hollow with wine.

🍷 *Opt for a robust pinot noir, like a mature Burgundy, if your Langres is very ripe. However, if it is still young and mild, choose a lighter, buttery Burgundy-style chardonnay, like Saint-Aubin, or Champagne.*

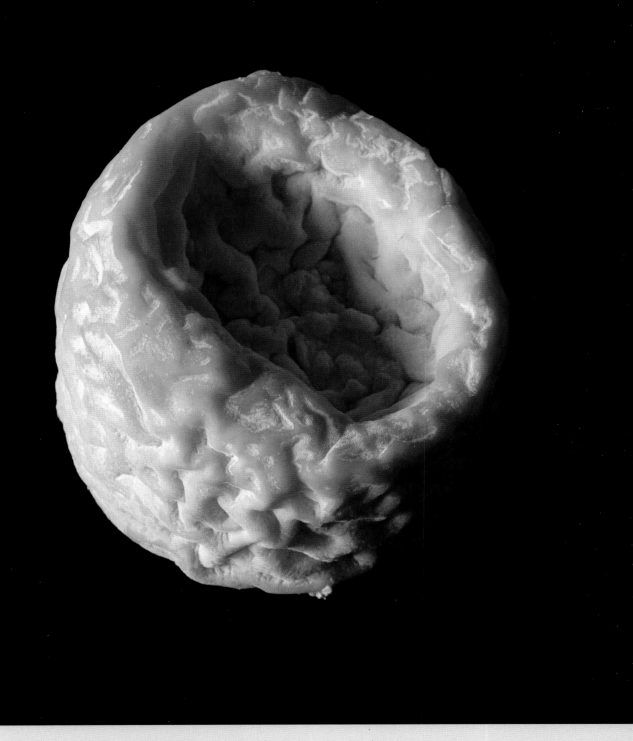

"This cheese isn't just attractive, it is unique in its region. Its closest relatives are too distant to be comparable. Refrigerated transport has fortunately made it possible to export Langres outside its region. Today, cheesemongers have learned to store it at optimum conditions and sell it at its perfect delicate, creamy best, neither too young nor too old."

LIVAROT ^{AOC 1975}

♦

**Soft cheese
Washed rind**

SEASON

SPRING   SUMMER   FALL   WINTER

○ *Geography and Origin:* Originating in Normandy in the Middle Ages, Livarot was once known as *Angelot* and *Augelot,* referencing its region, the Auge. It finally took its name from its birthtown. Livarot found early fame and is the most-consumed cheese from Normandy, well ahead of its cousins Camembert and Pont l'Évêque. It was cited in Thomas Corneille's *Universal Dictionary of Geography and History* as early as 1708. It is molded and aged in five rings of dried bulrush, which hold the shape of the cheese, especially during *affinage.* In its early days, Livarot was a leaner cheese, made from half-fat milk; farmers would skim the cream to make butter. The lower fat content made it more liable to collapse. This is why it is also called the "poor man's meat." Today Livarot is exclusively made using milk from the Normande breed of cows.

○ *Choose the Best:* Livarot comes in four formats: *grand* Livarot (2½ to 3⅓ pounds), Livarot (1 to 1¼ pounds), *trois-quarts* Livarot (11 to 12 ounces) and *petit* Livarot (7 to 9½ ounces). Even if they have become superfluous, dried bulrush or paper rings are still used. Its orange to reddish rind should be moist and sometimes sticky to the touch. Its interior should be supple: to check the consistency of the interior, remove the cheese from its box and touch its sides. Livarot has a pronounced aroma and a slightly salty, grainy texture. It has a powerful flavor, creamy when young; revealing floral aromas with notes of straw, leather, cabbage, and garlic when mature.

○ *How to Serve:* Some like it cooked because of the delicious aromas of leather and smoked charcuterie that emanate from it. Try a Normandy quiche with Livarot. You may prefer to remove the rind, which tends to amplify its flavor.

/ ☞ / Its closest relative is Pont l'Évêque.

STORAGE: Eight to twelve days in the coldest section of the refrigerator. Remove from the refrigerator an hour before serving.

🍷 *While locals serve it with country cider, a sweet white chenin blanc from the Loire, a Bonnezeaux appellation for example, would work perfectly. Avoid red wines, which tend to compete with Livarot and never really find their place.*

"Readily recognizable, Livarot is a favorite among foodies and cheese lovers who like their cheeses full and fla-vorful. Avoid Livarot if the rind peels away from the interior—this is a sign of poor maturity. With a good Livarot, you'll get to discover a jewel of the French gastronomic crown."

MÂCONNAIS AOC 2006

◆

**Soft cheese
Natural rind**

SEASON

| SPRING | SUMMER | FALL | WINTER |

○ *Geography and Origin:* When winegrowers allowed their goats to graze in their vineyards, Mâconnais was born. It was an original and practical initiative: the goats' milk was used for food and their manure to fertilize the land. Furthermore the small cheeses produced made for the perfect snack. Today the cheese is made exclusively with goat's milk from the Poitevine or Alpine breeds. Its fame traveled with the wine.

○ *Choose the Best:* Mâconnais, also known as Chevroton de Mâcon or Cabrion de Mâcon, is a small cheese weighing 1¾ to 2¼ ounces. Its truncated cone forms because it is not turned during the early ripe-ning process. Its small size means it dries very quickly. Its interior ranges from white to a bluish hue when mature. It has a grassy aroma when fresh, and has more lactic aromas after affinage. The drier it is, the saltier it is on the palate.

○ *How to Serve:* It can be consumed fresh, half-dried, or dried. When dried and matured, serve it with a slice of bread with a thin layer of whole-grain Dijon mustard or blackcurrant preserve. It also makes the perfect aperitif.

/ ☞ / Its closest relative is Charolais.

STORAGE: Several weeks in the refrigerator in its original paper or, if you want to eat it dry, without paper on a plate.

🍷 *This cheese is delicious with local wines from the Mâcon region—primarily fruity chardonnays, gamays, and pinot noirs, whether white or red—depending on the degree of maturity. For young cheeses, opt for Mâcon-Villages, a Montagny, or Petit Chablis; Pouilly-Fuissé is perfect for aged Mâconnais.*

"Some people are reluctant to touch this cheese, shaped like an upside-down vase or stopper, because of its blue spots. These spots are totally natural and give the cheese its natural aromas. When I explain this to guests, the cheese tends to disappear fast!"

MAROILLES ^{AOC 1976}

◆

**Soft cheese
Washed rind**

SEASON

SPRING   SUMMER   FALL   WINTER

○ *Geography and Origin:* The history of Maroilles goes back to the seventh century, when monks from the powerful Abbey of Maroilles made a cheese they called *craquegnon*, possibly the ancestor of Maroilles, even if this cheese was less ripe and gentler in flavor. In the tenth century, the Bishop of Cambray asked his monks to let the cheese ripen for longer and Maroilles was born. Today the Confrérie du Maroilles fellowship's slogan is: *Honni soit qui, sans maroilles, prétend tenir table loyale!* (May he who claims to maintain a loyal table, without Maroilles, be ashamed!). Its terroir with its lush grasslands is responsible for this rich, flavorful cheese and its unique aroma.

○ *Choose the Best:* Maroilles is said to be the gentlest of the strong cheeses. While it is always square, there are several sizes: the quart (6⅓ ounces), the mignon or demi (12¾ ounces), the *sorbais* or *trois-quarts* (1¼ pounds), or the *quatre-quarts* (1½ pounds). The cheese should be brick red, a color that develops due to Brevibacterium linens and the wash used during *affinage*. Its rind should be smooth and glossy. Its interior is golden yellow and creamy and has a very characteristic countryside aroma that should not smell of ammonia. Its flavor may be gentle or robust, depending on its shape and ripeness, but never bitter. The smaller the size, the sooner the cheese ripens. Treat yourself to a one-hundred-day Maroilles—you'll be eternally grateful.

○ *How to Serve:* There are local classics like the famous Tarte au Maroilles, or serve with steak in a Maroilles sauce made with beer and crème fraîche—delicious! It also works well in gougères, as an aperitif.

/ ☞ / Its closest relative is *Vieux-Lille.*

STORAGE: Depending on its size and affinage, store in the refrigerator. To catch it at its best, consume ninety days after production.

🍷 *Given the* terroir, *choose a good northern beer or cider. Be careful with red wines, which seldom pair well with soft, washed rind cheeses. Opt only for a mature red with soft tannins: classic Bordeaux, like Saint-Emilion grand cru, Fronsac, Côtes-de-Castillon, etc. In terms of white wines, opt for Gewurztraminer Vendanges Tardives or Vouvray Moelleux, ideal for the tangy, salty flavors of Maroilles.*

"The French movie, *Welcome to the Sticks*—a comedy about northern folk and their local customs—turned this cheese into a best-seller. I still have to drum into clients that Maroilles has to be eaten when mature. The aroma might well surprise but inside the cheese is very different. Originally this region did not permit the sale of the cheese until it was at least one hundred days old."

MONT D'OR
OR VACHERIN DU HAUT-DOUBS AOC 1981

◆

**Soft cheese
Washed rind**

SEASON

SPRING   SUMMER   FALL   WINTER

○ *Geography and Origin:* We know that Louis XV was a huge fan but dating it any further back is difficult. We know that the pastures of the Jura were first cleared for grazing in the tenth century. The hills, however, were home to the production of huge wheels of cheese, more practical given the amount of milk available. In late summer, the herds would come down to the plain where the herds' milk yields were lower, producing smaller-sized cheeses. It is around this period that Mont d'Or possibly came into being. The French version differs from the Swiss version because the French cheese uses raw rather than thermized milk. Mont d'Or is produced from August 15 to March 15 with the raw milk of Montbeliard and Simmental cows.

○ *Choose the Best:* Mont d'Or is sold in round boxes made of spruce wood and the cheese is wrapped in a strip of spruce bark, which gives it a unique flavor. There are several formats (1, 1¾, and 3 pounds) and it is only available in the fall and winter. It has a cream-colored, wrinkled rind with orangey pink and white blooms, depending on *affinage*. The interior is a rich, creamy, oozing ivory white. The more wrinkled it is, the riper it is. The undulating rind is caused by the cheese's mold that is larger than the box the cheese is sold in.

○ *How to Serve:* Place the box in a hot oven, like a fondue, and when crisp, golden, and bubbling serve with potatoes and garlic croutons. When very creamy, spoon onto good crusty bread.

/ 🐾 / Its closest relative is Reblochon.

STORAGE: Three weeks in a cool place.

🍷 *Pair with regional wines: a dry white Jura, Côtes-du-Jura, Arbois-Pupillin or Etoile. An Alsace Pinot-Noir also makes for an excellent choice.*

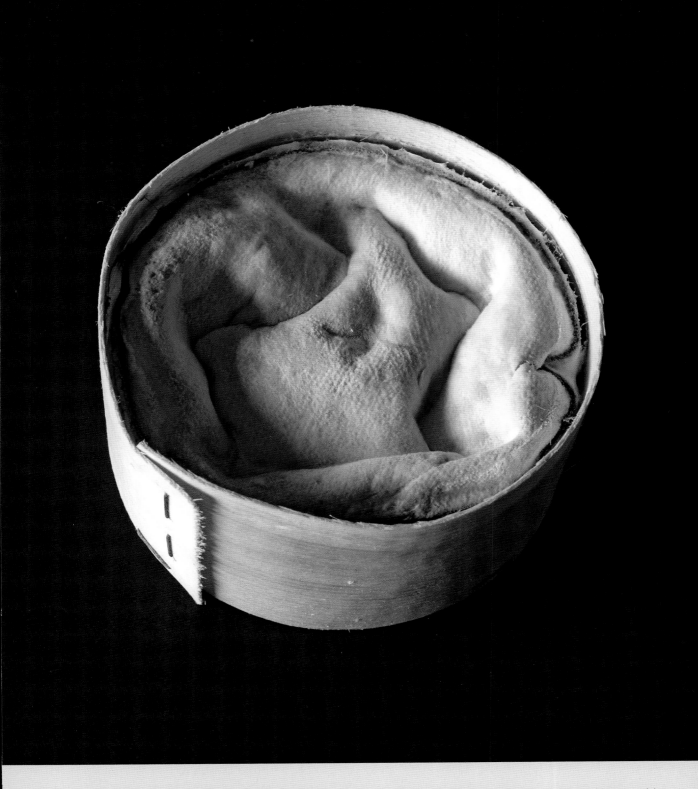

"If you don't know Mont d'Or, it's time to discover it! Rich and creamy, it is the perfect winter warmer. Hot or cold, it never fails to delight. Make sure to scrape the spruce-bark strip around it: this is the most fragrant and flavorful part. French Mont d'Or or Swiss Mont-d'Or—the choice is yours!"

MORBIER

◆

**Pressed
Uncooked**

SEASON

SPRING   SUMMER   FALL   WINTER

○ *Geography and Origin:* According to legend, Morbier was an accident that was caused by bad weather. Inclement conditions prevented farmers from transporting their milk to the *fruitière*, the cooperative where Comté is made. So, rather than lose their milk, the farmers poured it into a vat and sprinkled ashes on top to ward off insects. The next day, they would pour their new milk harvest on top. Others meanwhile say that Morbier was produced from surplus Comté curds. Cheese production in the Doubs and Jura region is recorded in the eighteenth century, and available writings mention a cheese with a "creamier pâte [...] with a blue vein through the middle." It was only in the following century that Morbier was named after the Jura town where it is produced. Today it is manufactured using only fresh milk in one batch and the ashes have been replaced by charcoal, which does not affect the taste of the cheese.

○ *Choose the Best:* Morbier is a flat wheel, 3 inches high with a weight between 11 to 17 pounds. It bears a casein label like Comté. Its light gray-beige, sometimes orange-ish, rind is smooth and natural. The narrow black line runs through the middle of the whole slice. The pale yellow interior may have a few small holes. It is a cheese with a pronounced, fruity, even caramel-vanilla aroma when mature.

○ *How to Serve:* Morbier is a cheese that needs no bread accompaniment. I advise parents to develop their children's taste for cheese with Morbier, as children love its light buttery flavor. In winter, it is perfect in a raclette.

/ 🖘 / Its closest relative is a young Vacherin Fribourgeois.

STORAGE: Two to three weeks in a cold, dry place, but not in the salad crisper of the refrigerator, which is too damp. Store on the warmest shelf of the refrigerator in its original wrapping paper. Remove from the refrigerator an hour before serving.

🍷 *Serve a young Morbier with a light, fruity Jura red of the poulsard grape variety. For more mature Morbier, go for a more robust Burgundy such as Rully, Mercurey, Bourgogne-Hautes-Côtes-de-Nuits, or Hautes-Côtes-de-Beaune. A local Vin d'Arbois or Jura white is also a safe bet.*

"Morbier is instantly recognizable because of the dark line down the center. This thin charcoal layer has no effect on flavor. In terms of value for money, Morbier is unbeatable and is always made with raw milk. When tender and aromatic, with notes of butter, vanilla, and caramel, Morbier is truly excellent."

MUNSTER
OR MUNSTER-GÉROMÉ ^{AOC 1969}

◆

**Soft cheese
Washed rind**

SEASON

SPRING   SUMMER   FALL   WINTER

○ *Geography and Origin:* Munster, it is said, was invented when in 660 Benedictine monks from Italy and Ireland settled at the foot of Mount Hohneck, on the east side of the Vosges Mountains between Alsace and Lorraine. The town that grew up nearby was named Munster, from the Latin *monasterium*. The cheese created by the monks became Munster when its recipe was shared with and gradually adopted by the local population. Munster is also known as Munster Géromé, in reference to the town of Gérardmer, on the other side of Vosges, which is also known as Géromé in the patois of Vosges. When the herds returned to their valleys, the cattle herdsmen would pay their tithes to the religious and political owners of the summer pastures; this they would do in both Gérardmer and Munster, so the tradition of the two names stuck.

○ *Choose the Best:* Munster is a flat wheel of cheese in two sizes, large and small (1 or ¼ pound). When young, its rind is orange and its texture supple. With age it turns a rustier color and its interior becomes creamier. Do not be put off by its odor, which is much stronger than its flavor. In the region, it is eaten fresher and white; outside of the region a more mature variety is preferred. This is for historical reasons: transport by horse and cart was slow, so by the time Munster arrived in Paris or Bordeaux, it was much riper.

○ *How to Serve:* Munster is best at the end of the meal. It is suggested you serve it with cumin seeds, for their digestive virtues. A Munster, cumin, and bacon cake makes a great aperitif: delicious and original!

/ ☞ / Its closest relative is Pont l'Évêque.

STORAGE: Eight to fifteen days on the warmest shelf of the refrigerator in its original wrapping paper. If too sticky, refrigerate without its wrapping paper and turn from time to time so that it dries on both sides. Remove from the refrigerator at least an hour before eating.

🍷 *Naturally because of the region a Gewurztraminer is perfect: a drier variety for young Munster, and Vendanges Tardives for a mature cheese. Munster also works perfectly with beer. Avoid red wine or opt for a medium-bodied red. Pairing with red wine is a risky business, though. You have been warned!*

"Many have suffered the woes of a long car journey with a ripening, unfettered Munster in their trunks. With its pronounced, balanced aromas, a moment with a fine Munster is one of life's true joys. Avoid if it is too moist or if it has aromas of cabbage and potato."

NEUFCHÂTEL AOC 1969

◆

**Soft cheese
Bloomy rind**

SEASON

SPRING   SUMMER   FALL   WINTER

○ *Geography and Origin:* There are no documents that record the exact origins of Neufchâtel; it has no official birth certificate. It is probably one of the oldest cheeses from Normandy, part of an ancestral cheese-making tradition that includes Bondons and Angelots. Toward 1543, its name was mentioned for the first time in the accounts of the Saint-Amand Abbey in Rouen. According to legend, the heart shape came about so that local girls could offer them to the English soldiers with whom they had sympathized. It was only in the nineteenth century that, with the development of its affinage, Neufchâtel met fame when Napoleon I tasted it on his passage through the region and was delighted with the taste.

○ *Choose the Best:* The cheese comes in six different forms: log, brick, square, double log, heart (its emblematic form), and large heart, the weights of which vary between 3½ ounces and 1⅓ pounds, depending on the model selected. Each shape has unique flavors and aromas; the smallest naturally ripen sooner than the largest. Neufchâtel has a fine white, bloomy rind with a fine velvety down, which turns golden depending on its state of maturity. The interior is firm and creamy and over time becomes more supple and elastic, but never runny. While saltier depending on the seasons, it always has a pronounced but gentle milky flavor. At cheese stalls, *fermier* Neufchâtel is presented on a straw mat, unwrapped, and is then packaged by the cheesemonger. Dairy Neufchâtel is presented in paper packaging or in a box.

○ *How to Serve:* Because of its slightly salty taste, serve Neufchâtel with blackberries, raspberries, or redcurrants. Try cooking with Neufchâtel as well—such as a Neufchâtel sauce with steak. It is a cheese full of surprises.

/ ☞ / Its closest relatives are Carré Frais *demi-se*l de Normandie or Chaource Champenois.

STORAGE: Eight to ten days in its original packaging beneath a glass cheese dome or on the warmest shelf in the refrigerator.

🍷 *Local farmstead sparkling cider is the obvious choice. You can also try fruity wines like Côtes du Rhône or a Loire red. The Loire red you choose will depend on the maturity of the cheese; from least to most mature try Saumur, Chinon, Anjou, Bourgueil, etc.*

"It is often known as the *Cœur de Neufchâtel*, in honor of its unique shape. This cheese is the pride of its region and is a big hit among many, maybe because it is pliable and gentle. The more you taste, the more you want. Its slightly saltier taste is quite normal and works perfectly with its creamy flavor and texture."

OSSAU-IRATY AOC 1980

◆

**Pressed
Uncooked**

SEASON

SPRING   SUMMER   FALL   WINTER

○ *Geography and Origin:* Its name comes from a fusion between its two sites of production in the valley of Ossau (Béarn) and the beech forest of Iraty (Basque country). It is first recorded in the first century; the Latin writer Martial talks of the sale of cheeses from the Pyrenees in Toulouse markets. It then reappears in manuscripts in the fifteenth century, when it was used for bartering and constituted the shepherd's main income. It gave its name to the famous Ossau-Iraty cheese route, a trail to some ninety producers to discover their terroir and expertise, acknowledged as one of France's "unique taste experiences."

○ *Choose the Best:* Its rind is thick, ranging from orange-yellow to ash gray. Its interior is ecru, smooth, firm, and creamy. Its flavor ranges from gentle to refined, depending on the pasture and length of maturity. The odor should be animal with a hint of lanolin. Good Ossau-Iraty is neither too salty nor its texture too woolly. It exists in raw milk, thermized, and pasteurized versions. Its iron-branded mark indicates the farmer's initials, a guarantee of provenance, manufacturing techniques, and thus quality. Ossau-Iraty is made with milk from ewes of Basco-béarnaise, Redhead, or Black-faced Manech breeds. There is a slight difference between the cheeses from Ossau and Iraty: Ossau cheeses are more tender and rounder, with small holes and more pronounced notes of ewe's milk; Iraty cheeses are drier and more angular with notes of hazelnut, hay, and prairie flora. When more mature, Iraty cheeses begin to show their more virile nature.

○ *How to Serve:* The cheese will develop all its aromas when finely sliced. Try it with black cherry preserve or fresh fruit. It can also be cooked: try Orloff roast pork, where the roast is first sliced then fine slivers of cheese and bacon are placed between the slices. Magnificent!

/ 🖝 / Its closest relatives are Idiazabal or Roncal.

STORAGE: If whole, it can be aged for several months in cool cellar-like conditions. If already cut, store for three weeks in the refrigerator. To limit waste, cut it on alternate sides each day, so that the rind does not re-form.

🍷 Opt for a lively, dry regional white wine, a Jurançon or Irouléguy, according to affinage: if the cheese is young, go for a sweet white wine; if more robust, choose a more full-bodied wine. Among reds, you will find an aged Madiran or Irouléguy work perfectly with the matured Ossau-Iraty.

"Like Beaufort, it is difficult to find a good Ossau-Iraty. As its name suggests, it has two versions. Traveling the region, you'll be sure to notice the difference between the Béarn and Basque country versions, Ossau and Iraty. One is tender and round, while the other is dry and spicy. Feel free not to have a preference!"

PÉLARDON AOC 2000

◆

**Soft cheese
Natural rind**

SEASON

SPRING	SUMMER	FALL	WINTER

○ *Geography and Origin:* While Pliny the Elder was already singing the praises of Languedoc cheeses in Antiquity, it was only in the eighteenth century that the name *Péraldou* first appeared in the records of the Cévennes. Depending on the village, Pélardon had different names—including *paraldon, pélardou, pérau-dou*—before Pélardon finally won out in the nineteenth century. If the cheese took a long time to develop, it was because the goat was considered to be the "poor man's cow" and goat's milk cheeses were not deemed worthy of the tables of the well-to-do. For a long time they kept their *fromage de ménage* (household cheese) status. The small size did not help and transport was difficult. So for many generations, the Pélardon was confined to its immediate local region. Today it is made from the milk of Alpine, Saanen, and Rove goats and gets to travel much more!

○ *Choose the Best:* The Pélardon should look like a small disk with rounded edges. After eleven days of ripening its rind is white and slightly wrinkled with some small yellow spots. Its creamy interior is white to ivory with a smooth and even texture, emanating aromas of goat's milk and hazelnuts. If ripened beyond three weeks the interior becomes brittle and the flavor more piquant. Its dry, beige rind turns almost blue if ripened for longer and its goat flavors become more concentrated.

○ *How to Serve:* Serve as an aperitif or a starter on a mixed leaf salad, broiled on toast, and drizzled with acacia honey (for those who like a sweet touch with their savories), or slice off fine shavings when dry. Pélardon is an ideal cheese for snacks, either served with or without alcoholic beverages. It makes for a perfect filler in the fall when served with walnuts and other dried fruits.

/ ☞ / Its closest relative is Rocamadour, and, surprisingly, not Picodon.

STORAGE: Store for several days to several weeks depending on affinage. The older Pélardon becomes, the more pronounced its flavor. Above all, do not wrap it in plastic; store it unwrapped on a plate in the refrigerator, otherwise it ferments.

🍷 *Pair a young Pélardon with a light, fruity southern wine: a Costières de Nîmes, a Côtes du Vivarais, or a Côtes du Rhône. For more mature cheeses, opt for more robust wines: Saint-Chinian, Faugères, Gigondas, or Patrimonio.*

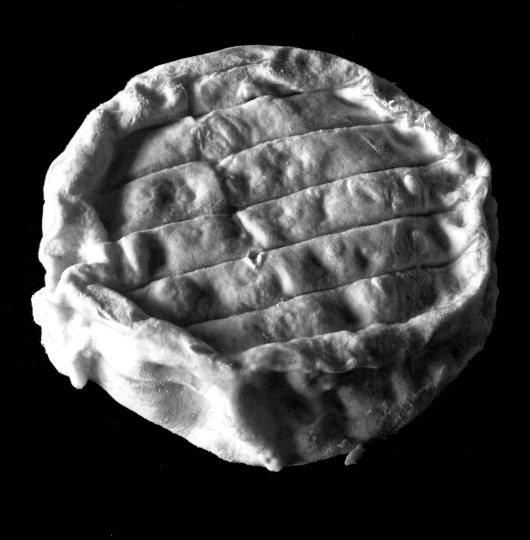

"The Pélardon is a regional wonder. At its frequent best it is creamy and irresistible, and you won't even want to eat it with bread: children love it this way, which is saying something, and many parents use it to develop their kids' gastronomic sensitivities. Watch out for Pélardons with gray spots on the rind: the quality might be compromised; choose it white and soft."

PICODON

AOC 1983

◆

Soft cheese
Natural rind

SEASON

SPRING SUMMER FALL WINTER

○ *Geography and Origin:* Very little information exists about this characterful little cheese, so typical of the Drôme and Ardèche regions. It has long been an integral feature of daily life here and one old regional saying states that: "A kiss without a beard has no more taste than a Picodon without salt." Until 1937, the Dieulefit-Montélimar train, which transported the cheese from the depths of the countryside to the main-line station in town, was known as "Le Picodon." Every summer the cheese has its own festival in the Drôme village of Saoû. Its name comes from "pico," local patois for "piquant." It is exclusively made with milk from goats of the white Saanen and Alpine Chamoissé breeds, who have had to acclimate to the hotter, more arid climate of the Rhône valley.

○ *Choose the Best:* Picodon is a small, irregular disk, weighing 2 ounces (1½ ounces for the Dieulefit version). Its fine rind ranges in color from white to pale yellow and is sometimes speckled with blue mold. Its interior is white or yellow with an even, smooth, never runny, texture. It should be cut cleanly with a knife. It has a very characteristic pronounced goat's cheese flavor with earthy and hazelnut notes. In Dieulefit, the Picardon ripened for more than one month and regularly washed. Its taste is stronger and tangier with a drier, even brittle texture.

○ *How to Serve:* Taste Picodon on its own, unaccompanied, or with a drizzle of olive oil and a single anchovy.

/ ☞ / Due to its pronounced flavor, its closest relative is a mature, dried Crottin de Chavignol.

STORAGE: When aged three weeks, store at a mild temperature so that it grows and develops. If already dry, store in the refrigerator for up to two weeks.

🍷 *A fresh Côtes du Rhône is perfect: grenache and syrah grape varieties with their red fruit and blackberry notes work perfectly with a Picodon Dieulefit and create a combination full of vitality. You can also taste it with a local wine: red Châtillon-en-Diois for a young Picodon and a white Crozes-Hermitage for a matured cheese. You can never go wrong with local wine!*

"Cheese lovers adore the piquancy of this cheese. While the Dieulefit variety is harder to come by, other local Picardons are readily available among French cheesemongers (in the US, however, even these are rare). They are at their best when their texture is brittle and their flavors at their most piquant and goaty."

PONT-L'ÉVÊQUE ^{AOC 1972}

◆

**Soft cheese
Washed rind**

SEASON

SPRING SUMMER FALL WINTER

○ *Geography and Origin:* Created near Caen in the twelfth century by Cistercian monks, this cheese was first made in a multitude of forms depending on the molds at the cheesemaker's disposal. In the fifteenth century, Normandy cheeses, known collectively as angelots, were the most reputed in the kingdom; Pont l'Évêque was among them. In the seventeenth century, a Norman poet, Hélie Le Cordier, wrote a poem about the cheese, which has become famous in the region: "Everybody loves it equally as it is made with such art that, old or young, it is only cream." Sold in the marketplace of Pont l'Évêque, the cheese took on the name of the small Normandy town. At the time, it was common practice to enrich the milk with cream to make an even more sumptuous cheese and only sell the best. Henceforth, Pont l'Évêque developed a reputation for quality.

○ *Choose the Best:* Pont l'Évêque comes in four formats: *grand* (maximum 3½ pounds), Pont l'Évêque (12 ounces), *petit* (minimum 6 ounces), and the *demi*. The most typical is the 12-ounce format. The cheese's original square shape differentiates it from its close relative, Livarot. Its smooth, yellow to orange rind is slightly plump. Its interior is tender, creamy, and salty, never dry or too runny, and it has notes of fruit and hazelnuts. It may appear to have a bloomier rind when it resembles Camembert; others say it has a washed rind because it resembles Livarot. Whatever its appearance, the rind is eminently edible and flavorful. The most important thing is to eat it when creamy and ripe right to the center.

○ *How to Serve:* Try baking pieces of Pont l'Évêque in rolls of broiled eggplant. Or add it to a lentil velouté. For the adventurous, make your own Pont l'Évêque ice cream and serve on stewed apples flambéed with Calvados.

/ ☞ / Its closest relative is, obviously, Livarot, but it has a family resemblance to Camembert de Normandie.

STORAGE: Eight to fifteen days. If ripened, store in its original paper and box. If not totally ripe, leave it in its box (like Camembert) and set aside at room temperature, remembering to turn it regularly.

🍷 *Like all characterful cheeses, Pont l'Évêque is difficult to pair with wine. Local Normandy cider always works. You can also try Loire or Burgundy wines like Bouzy, Bourgueil, or Pomerol, or a mature, robust wine like Vacqueyras, Gigondas, and Lirac. A sweet Chenin Blanc from Coteaux du Layon is also original. Try it, you'll be surprised!*

"Pont l'Évêque is still relatively unknown across France, and generally terra incognita for foreign palates, but it always piques newcomers' curiosity. When it is good it is very good. When you get to know it, it is one of the brightest lights of the French cheese landscape."

POULIGNY-SAINT-PIERRE ^{AOC 1972}

◆

**Soft cheese
Natural rind**

SEASON

SPRING   SUMMER   FALL   WINTER

○ *Geography and Origin:* The truncated pyramid form of this cheese is said to be based on the bell tower of the Pouligny-Saint-Pierre church. It is produced in the Brenne nature reserve in the south of the Berry region, one of the smallest grazing grounds compared to other cheese appellations. The area is unique for its small lakes and its flora dominated by cherry trees, heath, and sainfoin, which give the goat's milk, and thus the cheese, its characteristic fragrance. We know little of its origins, apart from the fact that goat's cheese was already being produced in the area in the eighteenth century. As a result, we might readily conclude that an early form of Pouligny-Saint-Pierre was already among those lucky cheeses.

○ *Choose the Best:* Its shape is readily recognizable. Pouligny-Saint-Pierre exists in large and small formats (9 ounces and 5 ounces). Its white to ivory interior is smooth, homogenous, and supple to the touch. Its surface is generally wrinkled and its dried grass and goat's milk odor is never too strong. The more it ages, the more blue spots appear. It has a broad range of flavors, depending on age. When young it is fresh and light on the palate. When it ripens it has a much more powerful character. It is particularly sought after when a delicious thick layer of cream forms beneath its rind.

○ *How to Serve:* For an appetizer try cheese skewers, alternating cherry tomatoes, cucumber, and smoked ham. It works well with walnut bread or in a salad seasoned with walnut oil.

/ ☞ / Its closest relative is Chabichou du Poitou.

STORAGE: One to three weeks. If very creamy, place it on a plate in the refrigerator, turning frequently.

♀ *A white sauvignon, like Reuilly, Quincy, Sancerre, Pouilly Fumé, or Bordeaux sec, a dry rosé like Touraine, and Coteaux-du-Vendômois are the easiest accompaniments. Their freshness and vivacity work well with the gently goaty, walnut aromas.*

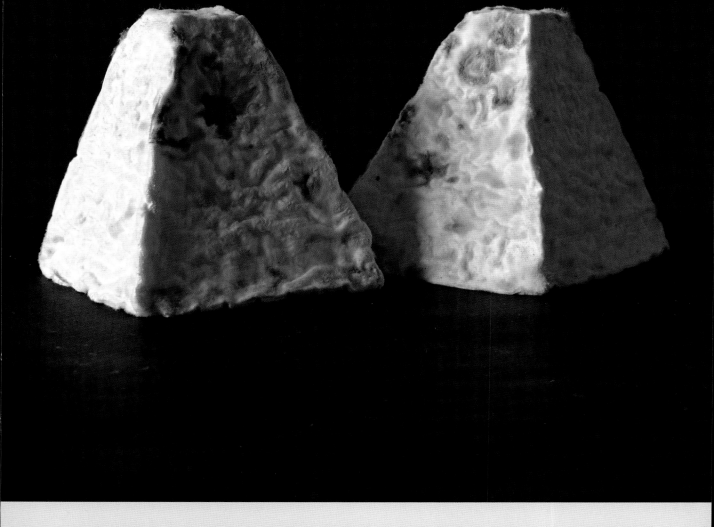

"Pouligny-Saint-Pierre always looks majestic on the platter. I only ever sell it whole. Cutting it in half would be a sacrilege. As it keeps well, you can store it for up to fifteen days after opening—you'll enjoy the difference in flavors as it ripens. I like it however it comes: dry or creamy."

REBLOCHON DE SAVOIE AOC 1958

◆

**Uncooked
Pressed**

SEASON

SPRING   SUMMER   FALL   WINTER

○ *Geography and Origin:* The origins of Reblochon date back to the Middle Ages when landowners—monks or nobles—had the right to tax their serfs' milk in proportion to production. So, farmers came up with a tax-reduction plan: when they milked their cows they would leave milk in the udder. They delivered the first yield to the inspector when he visited. Then when he left they would milk the cows again, a practice known in their patois as "reblocher," meaning "milking the udder a second time." The second yield was less abundant but creamier, perfect for cheesemaking. Until the mid-twentieth century, Reblochon remained a small-scale local cheese; it met with commercial success as winter sports developed and railways were introduced into the Savoie mountains.

○ *Choose the Best:* Reblochon is a flat wheel, roughly 5½ inches in diameter, with a smooth, yellow-orange rind flecked with dry white foam when well ripened. Its soft, creamy, smooth interior ranges from yellow to ivory. It is sold whole or in halves. Look out for the green casein label on a dairy Reblochon or the green casein label on the fermier Reblochon. Before packaging it is placed on a thin spruce wood tray, known as a "faux fond" (false bottom), which controls its humidity and helps it to ripen. A good Reblochon should have at least four to five weeks affinage. It is ready when it begins to "smell of cheese," emanating aromas of fresh grass and hazelnuts, while developing its rich pliable texture. Avoid over-ripened and overtly pungent Reblochon.

○ *How to Serve:* The perfect mountain dish, *tartiflette*, a gratin of potatoes, bacon, onions, and Reblochon, naturally calls out for Reblochon. Cooked Reblochon also works well with Savoyard buckwheat crozet pasta, or baked in flaky pastry or on a pizza. It is one of the cheeses best eaten alone with its rind: its flavors and textures are a delight even for the most delicate palates. Try serving with poppy seed or raisin bread.

/ ☞ / Its closest relative is Saint-Nectaire.

STORAGE: Two to three weeks in the refrigerator with its spruce tray (sold with the cheese), which protects the rind from humidity. The rind should not be sticky.

 Try a fruity red or a supple dry white wine.

"It is one of France's best-known cheeses because it is associated with the tartiflette. Reblochon also evokes all the memories of skiing holidays in the Savoie and Haute-Savoie—times of fun, friendship, and festivity, when rich, calorific, cheese-laden dishes are so very welcome as fuel for facing the snow-clad slopes."

RIGOTTE
DE CONDRIEU AOC 2009

◆

**Soft cheese
Natural rind**

SEASON

SPRING   SUMMER   FALL   WINTER

○ *Geography and Origin:* The tales of Rigotte de Condrieu's origins are legion. In one version, it is said that, in the nineteenth century, Condrieu market sold a cheese produced in the local Pilat Mountains, which took its name from the mountain streams, known as *rigols* or *rigots*. Another version states that it arrived when the Romans settled in Isère, having chased out the Allobroges. They passed on a cheesemaking technique using *recuite*—a starter culture of enzymes and bacteria—hence the names *rigotte* and ricotta. What we do know is that goat farming has been in the area since the seventh century and the rich variety of flora in the Pilat Mountains has always produced delicious cheeses. Today Alpine and Saanen goat breeds produce this small cheese with its subtle, fragrant aroma.

○ *Choose the Best:* When mature, Rigotte de Condrieu should resemble a small wheel 1½ to 2 inches in diameter. It has a rind dappled with ivory, white, and blue mold, depending on the state of maturity. Its texture is fine and firm with a smooth, dry interior. It has a slightly tangy flavor with aromas of hazelnut, mushroom, and butter.

○ *How to Serve:* Try a clafoutis with zucchini and Rigotte, or wrap the cheese in filo pastry parcels with caramelized apple.

/ ☞ / Its closest relatives are Chabichou du Poitou or Pouligny-Saint-Pierre.

STORAGE: May be stored wrapped in wax paper in the crisper drawer of your refrigerator for up to three weeks. Remove from the refrigerator several hours before eating. If storing for only several days, place in a corked stoneware pot in a cool place to mature gently.

🍷 *For a young cheese, opt for a dry white Rhône valley wine, such as Condrieu, Ventoux, Chardonnay, or Côtes-du-rhône. For a mature cheese, opt for powerful reds like Côte-Rotie, Saint-Joseph, Crozes-Hermitage, or Minervois. On the palate, the cheese may initially present as robust, but a delicate balance of tangy goat's milk and red fruit and leather notes soon emerge.*

"This small raw-milk goat's cheese from the Pilat Mountains is hard to come by. Production is small and probably mainly consumed locally—which is a pity! This diminutive wonder, with its creamy heart, is one of the marvels of Lyon gastronomy."

ROCAMADOUR AOC 1996

◆

Soft cheese
Natural rind

SEASON

SPRING   SUMMER   FALL   WINTER

○ *Geography and Origin:* Rocamadour is part of the broader Cabécou family, a generic term for all goat's cheeses made within the vast area of the Massif Central to the Pyrenees foothills. Long called Cabécou de Rocamadour, it was renamed Rocamadour when it attained AOC labeling to pinpoint its production zone. It has been traced back to the fifteenth century when, like many cheeses of the time, it was produced by farmers to pay their tithes to the landowners of the region. The village of Rocamadour is located on the Way of Saint James, so the many pilgrims who flocked to the village have no doubt helped spread the cheese's reputation.

○ *Choose the Best:* This tiny 1¼-ounce disk is a mouthful in itself. Beneath its velvety white skin, its interior is creamy with gentle goat's milk flavors. When matured its natural rind may be speckled with blue spots and its flavor is more pronounced. On the palate, Rocamadour has light lactic and hazelnut aromas. When creamy, it delights the taste buds and makes one forget one's daily worries. When eaten dry, you'll find your senses are suddenly awakened and you can't help but instantly start talking about it.

○ *How to Serve:* Alone, Rocamadour is divine. But in cooking, there is a tendency in France to broil it and serve it on salad. Take the time instead to treat it right and it'll offer its best. Try it baked on flaky pastry or bread accompanied with a salad seasoned with walnut oil. Or treat yourself to a Mediterranean vegetable lasagna with Rocamadour.

/ ☞ / Its closest relative is Pélardon.

STORAGE: When ripe at the center and creamy, store for only a few days. If more mature, you can store for longer—its taste will become more pronounced and its texture firmer.

🍷 *Don't be taken in by its size. It might be small but it has huge character. It works wonders with both white and red wines. Try Sancerre or, if you fancy something sweeter, Coteaux du Layon. If you feel like a red wine, opt for Cahors or Beaujolais—lighter, fruity wines from the gamay or malbec grape.*

"Rocamadour is very often copied but never equaled. To catch it at its best, listen to your cheesemonger. If all they say is that it comes from the Lot region and is good in salads, then beware! Personally, I could talk about this tiny cheese for hours on end."

ROQUEFORT AO 1925 AOC 1975

◆

Blue cheese

SEASON

| SPRING | SUMMER | FALL | WINTER |

○ *Geography and Origin:* According to the Roquefort legend, a shepherd who was minding his flocks, and enjoying his lunch of fresh cheese and bread, was distracted by a young girl. He hid his humble meal in a fissure in a nearby cave (known locally as a *fleurine*). A few days later, when he returned, the bread and cheese had fused and Roquefort was born. The cheese is recorded to have been sold in Roman markets in Antiquity, but it was not until the eleventh century that the name Roquefort was adopted. Over the centuries, the cheese seduced its sovereign rulers, who protected its manufacture and caves. In the twentieth century, it developed world renown, becoming one of the most famous French cheeses. It is the first cheese to have received Appellation d'Origine (AO) status in 1925. Today the cheese can be made with milk from only the Lacaune breed and its black variety. It is aged in the caves of Roquefort-sur-Soulzon.

○ *Choose the Best:* Roquefort is always made with raw milk and is manufactured as a 5- to 6-pound wheel, which should have a certain moisture. Its interior is white to ivory and its blue-green veins should be well distributed in sufficient, but not excessive, quantities from the center to the edges. Roquefort should not taste too salty, tart, or bitter. The flavor should be smooth, leaving a pronounced fresh sensation in the mouth.

○ *How to Serve:* It is often recommended at the end of a meal because blue cheese floras are a digestive aid. But you can also enjoy Roquefort at any time of the day, served on a slice of thin bread. It is also highly suitable for cooking and it melts harmoniously into savory and sweet recipes—with pasta or chicken, in pies and cakes, soups and sauces, or mousses and dips.

/ ☞ / Its closest relative is Bleu des Causses, even though it is made from pasteurized cow's milk and does not have the same appearance.

STORAGE: As it is a "strong" blue cheese, store for eight to fifteen days in the refrigerator. Remove from the refrigerator just before serving: at room temperature its flavor is stronger and its texture more buttery.

🍷 *Choose a full-bodied red like Châteauneuf-du-Pape, Madiran, and Cahors. As an appetizer, eat with sweet liquoreux white wines like Sauternes, Monbazillac, Jurançon moelleux, Vin Jaune, gewurztraminer, an aged Banyuls, and even a white port.*

"Everything has been said about Roquefort, but I always find something new to say about its constant charm. It makes for the perfect pick-me-up: a quick snack of Roquefort spread on bread and I'm ready to go. First aid and survival kits everywhere should include a tender, flavorful Roquefort!"

SAINT-NECTAIRE ^{AOC 1955}

♦

**Pressed
Uncooked**

SEASON

SPRING   SUMMER   FALL   WINTER

○ *Geography and Origin:* Saint-Nectaire has its origins in the Middle Ages. It is recorded that farmers would pay their tithes with "rye cheese," and the ancestral method for ripening Saint-Nectaire once involved maturing it on rye wicker mats on the baked-earth farmhouse floor. Several centuries later, it was presented to the Sun King, Louis XIV, by the regional lord, Maréchal Henri de La Ferté-Senneterre, to whom it owes its name. Born in the harsh climate of central France, at an altitude of 2,500 to 5,000 feet, it has a luxuriant terroir, lush in wild flowers with great biodiversity.

○ *Choose the Best:* Saint-Nectaire comes with a very bloomy brown rind or a less bloomy pink-orange rind. Whether *fermier* (with its elliptical green casein label) or dairy (with its square green casein label), its rind is dappled with white, yellow, or red mold, depending on the state of maturity. This mold develops due to the breezes blowing through the ripening cellars and from regular brushing. The interior should be supple and creamy but never runny. It should have earthy odors with floral scents of forest flowers. On the palate, its taste is delicate yet surprisingly generous. Beneath its rustic exterior, it hides its subtle, noble qualities, recalling why it was such a big hit with Louis XIV. In its home region of Auvergne, the question that divides people is: which is best? The gray rind or the pink-orange rind? Naturally, they are both delicious. Outside the region, urbanites have a preference for it when its rind is black and furry with mold.

○ *How to Serve:* Eat with its rind when its interior is delicate and tender. Serve with or without bread, alone, or accompanied by grapes. Saint-Nectaire is divine however it comes.

/ ☞ / Its closest relative is Reblochon.

STORAGE: Two to three weeks. Store the black rind variety (which is drier than the type with the pink-orange rind) at warmer temperatures. Both should be stored beneath a glass cheese dome in their original wrapping paper.

🍷 *A Saint-Estèphe, Côtes du Rhône, or a Burgundy are perfect with this surprisingly urbane, mountain cheese. Pair with a light, fruity regional Côtes d'Auvergne. A light supple red wine would help to express the cheese's subtle aromatic range.*

"When I was a child, I hated Saint-Nectaire and I couldn't understand why my mother loved it so. Gradually I developed a taste for it and when I visited the ripening cellars I became truly aware of its excellence. It is one of our bestsellers year-round. Customers often talk about it while they're buying it."

SAINTE-MAURE-DE-TOURAINE AOC 1990

◆

Soft cheese
Natural rind

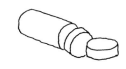

SEASON

SPRING   SUMMER   FALL   WINTER

○ *Geography and Origin:* Since the Moorish invasions in the seventh century, goat-rearing has been ever present in the Touraine region. It is said the recipe for Sainte-Maure-de-Touraine was passed on by Muslim women who remained in France after the retreat of the Umayyads at the Battle of Poitiers. Exclusively produced in the Touraine, the techniques were passed down from mother to daughter over time, improving all the while: until the twentieth century, goat-rearing and goat's cheese production was considered to be an exclusively female domain. Today Sainte-Maure-de-Touraine is made with goat's milk from the Alpine and Saanen goat breeds.

○ *Choose the Best:* True Sainte-Maure-de-Touraine is presented skewered with a dry stick of rye, which is a guarantee of quality. Another indicator of authenticity is the casein label identifying the cheesemaker. The oval AOP label is the final proof you are in the presence of a genuine Sainte-Maure-de-Touraine. The cheese has a truncated cone form and its cylinder narrows at one end. The gray-blue, dry, and bloomy rind should be neither moist nor sticky and should have no downy fur. The interior is white or ivory, and its texture soft and homogenous, never grainy or chalky. Its aroma is distinctly goaty but also has earthy notes of grass and hay with hints of hazelnut. On the palate, the cheese has a delectable balance of goat's milk and butter with a smooth, tender, creamy center. It is tasted fresh, *demi-affiné* (half-dry), or *affiné* (with a smooth brittle heart). It is best after one month of aging.

○ *How to Serve:* The rye stick is used to maintain the shape of Sainte-Maure-de-Touraine after its mold is removed. When it comes to serving, cut the cheese without cutting the stick. It is delicious with dried or fresh fruit, as well as pears, walnuts, prunes, and figs. Try a gratin of Sainte-Maure-de-Touraine with pears in syrup.

/ ☞ / Its closest relative is Valençay.

STORAGE: One to three weeks, depending on maturity. Whether fresh or dry, store in the refrigerator. If you wish to ripen it further, place it beneath a glass cheese dome at room temperature for several days until you find the flavor your looking for.

🍷 *With a young Sainte-Maure-de-Touraine, choose a dry white wine, like Touraine wine made with the chenin blanc grape. For a more mature cheese, opt for a sauvignon, like Touraine sauvignon, Sancerre, or Pouilly Fumé. Red wine is difficult to pair with this cheese. If you cannot resist, opt for a light red, such as Saumur, and serve with a young cheese.*

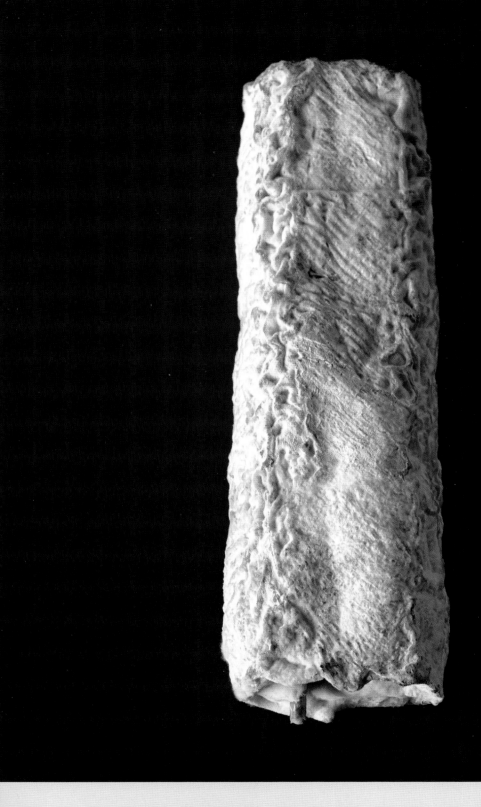

"A cheese readily recognizable from its rye stick through the middle. It is rare that clients ask for the cheese to be cut in half."

SALERS AOC 1961

◆

**Pressed
Uncooked**

SEASON

SPRING   SUMMER   FALL   WINTER

○ **Geography and Origin:** The history of this ancestor to Cantal goes back to the Middle Ages, perhaps even before. Salers was first made during the transhumance in burrons, the cowherds' shacks. Today it enjoys farmstead production and there are ninety remaining producers in the region maintaining the Salers tradition. Salers is an exclusively fermier handmade cheese, so it can be hard to find at French market stalls: it is said that "90 farmers equals 90 Salers!" The cheese is produced during the grazing season, April 15 to November 15, with milk from Salers cows. The cow is milked twice a day with the veal calf present, otherwise the Salers cow refuses to yield her milk.

○ **Choose the Best:** Traditionally produced cheeses have their own special markings. On the top, the cheese is imprinted with the label: *Tradition Salers* or *Salers Salers*, with an ink-stamped muslin strip featu-

ring two cows' heads. The rind is thick with red and orange blooms. Its interior is firm, ivory to yellow in color, and has the complexion of dry rock. Its subtle fruity flavor comes from the diversity of the Cantal region's grasslands, which feature such fragrant succulent flavors as gentian and blueberries that are passed on into the milk. In the mouth the interior crumbles, revealing lactic aromas with a slightly bitter tang. The best month to eat it is in September.

○ **How to Serve:** Savor without an accompaniment. Its richness and complexity suffice. You could also serve it for brunch with apples, cherry preserves, *viande des grisons* (fine slices of dried, cured beef), and bread. It is fun to have tasting sessions with friends to explore the differences between Cantal, Laguiole, and Salers. For the best comparison, choose them at similar points of maturity.

/ ☞ / Its closest relatives are vieux Cantal or Laguiole Grand Aubrac.

STORAGE: Several weeks in the refrigerator in its packaging. Avoid humidity, which would turn it blue. Remove from the refrigerator for an hour before serving.

🍷 *It is difficult to find the right balance between a fruity red, which is no match for this characterful mountain heavyweight, and more robust red wines, which risk being too tannic and will only compete with its flavor. Salers is particularly sensitive to the structure of wines. Whether red or white, make sure it is round and sufficiently aged. Adjust your choices depending on the age of the cheese. A Côtes-de-Provence for a young Salers, a Châteauneuf-du-Pape for a Salers aged six months.*

"I particularly love Salers. I love its imposing mass, its speckled rind, and the interior resembling dry rock. When you pull it with your fingers the interior crumbles, releasing the aromas of the wild flora of the Cantal peaks. All the trials and treats of the Cantal volcanoes, their luxuriant vegetation, and their harsh climate are contained in this cheese."

SELLES-SUR-CHER ^{AOC 1975}

◆

**Soft cheese
Natural rind**

SEASON

SPRING   SUMMER   FALL   WINTER

○ *Geography and Origin:* Initially, goat herds in the region were too small to yield milk sufficient for commercial exploitation, and the cheese remained in the family. Expertise, techniques, and tips were passed down from mother to daughter. It was not until the nineteenth century that the cheeses known as *selles*—because they were molded in *faisselles*—began to develop and make a name for themselves. The nearest market town was Selles-sur-Cher, so naturally this became the cheese's name. In the past, it was sprinkled with ashes to ward off insects; today charcoal dust is used.

○ *Choose the Best:* Selles-sur-Cher is instantly recognizable from its flat, truncated disk shape (4 inches in diameter) with its beveled edges. When fresh it weighs 7 ounces, but when matured in a dry cave d'affinage, it weighs only 5 ounces. The slightest production error and the batch loses its AOP classification. The fine regular rind has surface mold and a blue charcoal tinge. During ripening, a white downy layer may appear. Firm to the touch, its rind conceals a white, homogenous, sometimes creamy interior. It has hazelnut aromas and is pliable on the palate.

○ *How to Serve:* Make a tapenade with Selles-sur-Cher and serve with a salmon carpaccio—it's a real treat. Or smear it on crackers with dried fruits.

/ ☞ / Its closest relative is Valençay.

STORAGE: One to three weeks. If not creamy, and you want to maintain this characteristic, store in the refrigerator. If you want it creamy, store beneath a glass cheese dome and leave to ripen at room temperature.

🍷 *Opt for a light regional red, such as Cheverny, Valençay, Saint-Nicolas-de-Bourgueil, Touraine, Saumur, or a dry sauvignon such as Pouilly Fumé, Sancerre, Reuilly, or Menetou-Salon. The fruity mineral notes of some whites combine deliciously with the goaty hazelnut nuances of this cheese.*

"For many, Selles-sur-Cher is an essential ingredient of any cheese platter. It is a feast for the eyes and appeals visually to cheese novices, who will ask if the rind should be eaten. The answer is naturally 'Yes!'—especially if you want to enjoy the creamy layer beneath the rind."

TOME
DES BAUGES AOC 2002

◆

**Pressed
Uncooked**

SEASON

SPRING   SUMMER   FALL   WINTER

○ *Geography and Origin:* Tome des Bauges originally was made with skimmed milk, after the cream had been removed to make butter. In 1807, the governor of the local town, Barante, classified it as "peasants' daily fodder." In order to differentiate it from the tommes of the region, and as a reference to the Savoyard word "toma," meaning "made in the *alpages*," the single "m" spelling of Tome de Bauges was adopted. For a long time Tomme de Savoie was a bigger seller, but today Tome des Bauges has gained the advantage, and is greatly sought after.

○ *Choose the Best:* Tome des Bauges is either *fermier* (green casein label) or dairy-produced (red casein label), and is sold whole or cut. The wheels are 8 inches in diameter. Its gray surface is covered in a natural downy bloom called the mucor. Its rind is granular, thick, and pitted. The interior is yellow to ivory, supple, and homogenous when young; firmer when matured. On the palate the texture is pliable with fruity aromas.

○ *How to Serve:* It is a marvel in a *croque-monsieur* or an omelet, but also combined with crudités or a salad. In Savoie, it often accompanies soup. In winter, it is delicious in a Savoyard fondue.

/ 🖘 / Its closest relative is Tomme de Savoie.

STORAGE: Two to four weeks, but not in the refrigerator if cut; its flavor is too delicate. If whole, however, it stores well for weeks in the refrigerator before cutting.

🍷 *At last a cheese that likes red wine. Choose round, fruity wines when young, such as Bordeaux, Premières-Côtes-de-Blaye, Côtes-de-Bourg, Bergerac, or Chinon), and more structured wines with ripened cheese (a Savoie mondeuse, Madiran, Châteauneuf-du-Pape, or Patrimonio).*

"A cheese for the initiated because many overlook it and associate it with its Savoyard cousin. I like this Tome a great deal—it is a simple, authentic old-school cheese, and it is always a great pleasure to cut into it to reveal the riches within."

VALENÇAY AOC 1998

♦

**Soft cheese
Natural,
ash-coated rind**

SEASON

SPRING SUMMER FALL WINTER

○ *Geography and Origin:* While the ancestors of this cheese date back to the Middle Ages, its pyramid was noticeably different to the cheese we know today. It is said the tip of the pyramid disappeared in the eighteenth century when French Foreign Minister Talleyrand decreed its form should be changed so as not to remind Napoleon of his recent defeat in Egypt. And so it came to resemble the bell tower of Valençay church. Today Valençay is made with the milk from Alpine and Saanen goat breeds.

○ *Choose the Best:* The cheese has two formats: 7¾ ounce and *petit-valençay*, 4 ounces. To comply with AOP regulations, a good Valençay has an even, truncated pyramid shape with clean, straight edges. Its sides should not be hemmed or bulging. Its color, including the base, should be a uniform blue-gray. Yellow and ashen white patches are not acceptable. The surface shows light, homogenous wrinkling, known as "vermiculation." Slicing in you discover a white, almost ivory interior (above all, not yellow), that is even and

without holes. The texture is neither moist nor brittle. Its rind should not separate from the cheese. The ripening process is essential and the interior should not become too runny beneath the rind. It has a tangy goat's milk smell, and earthy mushroom aromas, similar to the aromas of goat's milk. If it is odorless, it is not a good sign. To the taste it is neither bitter nor acid and should be neither too salty nor atypical. On the palate, it has pronounced, well-developed aromas and a firm, pliable texture. It should be neither runny nor dry.

○ *How to Serve:* Bake in the oven in flaky pastry parcels with honey. Baked, it is perfect in pies and gratins. On the end-of-meal cheese platter, serve with rye bread and dried fruits, or with a juicy pear and crusty bread.

/ ☞ / Its closest relative is Selles-sur-Cher.

STORAGE: One to three weeks. Turn regularly. If it becomes creamy, place in the refrigerator to stop the process. If pliable, store beneath a glass cheese dome at room temperature.

🍷 *Valençay always works well with local regional wines from Berry or Touraine, whether red, rosé, or a lively fruity white. For reds, opt for Valençay, Touraine, or Anjou; or, for whites, Valençay, Pouilly Fumé, and Sancerre.*

"Smaller and denser than the Pouligny-Saint-Pierre, it is a marvel of the truncated-pyramid goat's cheese varieties. To maintain its aromas, place it on one side for several hours, then switch sides to let each side breathe (without placing it on its top). This will ensure perfect, even ripening."

RECIPES

Dominique Bouchait's Selection

MEILLEUR OUVRIER DE FRANCE FAVORITES

FONDUE SAVOYARDE

PIERRE GAY – MOF CHEESEMONGER 2011

Serves 5

14 ounces Comté AOP, aged 18 to 24 months

14 ounces Alpes Suisses de L'Etivaz [AOP]

7 ounces Beaufort d'alpage AOP (summer Beaufort)

3½ ounces fermier Abondance [AOP]

1½ cups dry white wine from Savoie (apremont grape variety)

17½ ounces crusty country bread, cut into small cubes

1 egg

• Grate or slice each cheese and place in a medium saucepan, pour over the white wine, and heat on a brisk heat, stirring with a wooden spoon. Resist the temptation to add more wine; let the cheese absorb the wine first. The cheese should melt fairly quickly (5 to 7 minutes).

• When white foam appears on the surface, the fondue is almost ready. Light your fondue burner and invite your guests to dip the small chunks of bread into the gooey, cheesy sauce with fondue or other long forks.

• When the fondue is almost finished, add whatever bread is left to the cheese and break in an egg, stirring with a wooden spoon.

Suggestion: Serve the fondue with charcuterie and a green salad. Accompany with white wine, especially of the same type you used for the fondue.

BLEU DE TERMIGNON CRUMBLE WITH HONEY

JACQUES DUBOULOZ – MOF CHEESEMONGER 2004

Serves 4
4 slices good-quality bread
7 ounces Bleu de Termignon
Mountain or forest honey (pine honey)

• Lightly toast slices of doughy, crusty bread, and crumble the Bleu de Termignon on top.
• Drizzle honey over the cheese.
• Eat cold or place under the broiler and serve golden and sizzling.

Suggestion: This snack is even more delicious when the cheese is younger and not entirely blue. Its white crumbly interior brings a fresh tangy flavor. You can replace the honey with small pieces of blueberry fruit jelly.

BRILLAT SAVARIN
WITH DRÔME TRUFFLES

ÉTIENNE BOISSY – MOF CHEESEMONGER 2004

Serves 4
1 Brillat Savarin
½ ounce fresh truffle
9 tablespoons Mascarpone

• Using a cheese wire, cut the Brillat Savarin in thirds horizontally. You will have 3 rounds of cheese.
• Crush the fresh truffle with a fork and stir it into the mascarpone.
• Piece the cheese back together, spooning a layer of truffle-mascarpone mixture in between each round. Refrigerate for 24 hours.

Suggestion: Serve with a mixed leaf salad with hazelnut oil and toasted bread accompanied by a white Crozes-Hermitage.

CAMEMBERT DE NORMANDIE WITH CARAMELIZED PEARS

DOMINIQUE BOUCHAIT – MOF CHEESEMONGER 2011

Serves 4

4 Williams pears
1 tablespoon hazelnut butter
1 tablespoon sugar
1 Camembert de Normandie [AOP]
4 tablespoons crème fraîche

• Preheat the oven to 425°F using the broiler of your oven.
• Peel the Williams pears and slice into quarters. Fry them in the butter, then add the sugar, and continue heating until the sugar caramelizes.
• Cut the Camembert in half horizontally to make 2 rounds, then cut each round in half.

• Set 4 wide ramekins on a baking sheet. Place 4 pieces of pear and 1 tablespoon of crème fraîche in the ramekins. Place one piece of Camembert on top.
• Set in the oven, but keep an eye on the ramekins. The cheese should melt but not too much.
Suggestion: Serve with salad seasoned with walnut vinegar and a handful of toasted almonds.

BUTTERNUT SQUASH VELOUTÉ WITH CÉSAR RÉGALIS

DOMINIQUE BOUCHAIT – MOF CHEESEMONGER 2011

Serves 6

1 butternut squash
Vegetable stock
1 cup light cream
2 ounces César Régalis, cubed
Salt and freshly ground black pepper
12 slices of bread

• Peel the butternut squash and cut the flesh into cubes. Place the cubes in a medium saucepan and add vegetable stock to cover. Cook until a knife slides in easily, about 20 minutes. When ready, drain and blend into a purée. Add the cream and 1½ ounces of the blue cheese. Season with salt and pepper.

• Toast the slices of bread.
• Serve the velouté with a few cubes of Régalis on top and 2 slices of toasted bread on the side.

COMTÉ GOUGÈRES WITH PORCINI MUSHROOMS

LUDOVIC BISOT – MOF CHEESEMONGER 2015

Makes 16 gougères
16 porcini mushrooms • A drizzle of sunflower oil
Salt and freshly ground pepper • A drizzle of hazelnut oil
1 cup water • 9 tablespoons unsalted butter
1 cup flour • 4 eggs
3½ ounces grated Comté ᴬᴼᴾ

• Preheat the oven to 325°F. Line a baking sheet with parchment paper.
• Peel the porcinis and brush the caps beneath a drizzle of water. Arrange them on a dry cloth.
• Brown the mushrooms in a sauté pan with a little sunflower oil, then season with salt and pepper. Drizzle with hazelnut oil and set aside.
• Pour the water into a medium saucepan, then add the butter and a pinch of salt. Bring to a boil.
• Remove from the heat and add the flour. Beat with a wooden spoon until you obtain an even mixture that pulls away from the sides of the pot. Return the

pot to the heat and cook on low heat for 1 minute.
• Add the eggs, one at a time, to the flour mixture, stirring well between additions. Add the Comté and beat the mixture with a wooden spoon to form a smooth creamy batter.
• Coat each mushroom in the batter, making sure each is well coated. Place on the prepared baking sheet. Bake until the gougères are puffed and golden, 20 to 30 minutes. Serve hot or warm.
Suggestion: Serve with a white Côtes-du-Jura (savagnin grape variety) or a white Burgundy, like Pouilly-Fuissé.

JURA CROSTINI

MARC JANIN – MOF CHEESEMONGER 2015
FROMAGERIE JANIN – CHAMPAGNOLE (39)

Serves 4
4 thick slices crusty farmhouse bread • 14 ounces Comté AOP, aged 14 to 20 months
2 tablespoons crème fraîche • 3 tablespoons Jura white wine (savagnin grape)
1 pinch curry powder • 1 pinch freshly ground black pepper

• Preheat the broiler. Place the slices of bread on a baking sheet and lightly toast the bread (keep an eye on the bread so it doesn't burn). Turn the oven to 350°F.
• Grate the Comté.
• In a medium bowl, combine the Comté, crème fraîche, white wine, curry powder, and pepper.

• Spread the Comté mixture on the slices of bread and place on a baking sheet lined with parchment paper.
• Bake in the oven for 5 to 10 minutes at 350°F. Keep an eye on the cheese to make sure it turns a nice golden color on top.

CERVELLE DE CANUT

DIDIER LASSAGNE – MOF CHEESEMONGER 2007

Serves 4

17½ ounces drained raw milk fromage blanc

2 tablespoons olive oil

2 tablespoons crème fraîche

1 tablespoon cider vinegar

Chopped chives

Pinch salt

1 clove garlic, crushed

1 shallot, finely sliced

1 loaf crusty country bread

• Vigorously beat the ingredients together in a medium bowl.

• Cover with plastic wrap and let rest for 5 hours in the refrigerator.

• Spread on slices of bread.

OYSTER SOUFFLÉ
WITH MOLITERNO AL TARTUFO

DAVID GOMES – MOF FISHMONGER 2011

Serves 4

12 oysters • 1½ cups milk • 4 tablespoons unsalted butter

½ cup flour • 4 large eggs • Salt

5½ ounces Moliterno al Tartufo • Nutmeg

Freshly ground black pepper

• Preheat the oven to 350°F. Open the oysters, set them on a baking sheet, and bake them in the oven for 5 minutes in their shells.

• Place the milk in a small saucepan and warm over low heat. In a medium saucepan on medium heat, melt the butter, then add the flour and stir briskly for 1 minute. Gradually add the warm milk and whisk the mixture vigorously. Remove the pot from the heat.

• Separate the egg whites from the yolks. Add a pinch of salt to the whites and whip them into stiff peaks using a handheld blender or stand mixer.

• In a cold casserole, add the egg yolks, one at a time, then the grated cheese. Add a pinch of nutmeg and a pinch of black pepper. Do not add much salt, as the cheese is already sufficiently salty. Gently fold the whipped egg whites into the egg and cheese mixture.

• Coat the oysters in their shells with this mixture.

• Bake in the oven for 10 minutes. Serve immediately.

GREEN ASPARAGUS AND DUCK FOIE GRAS WITH COMTÉ COULIS AND VIN JAUNE MOUSSELINE

MICHEL ROTH – MOF CHEF 1991

Serves 4

16 green asparagus • Salt, Freshly ground black pepper
3½ ounces clarified butter • 8½ ounces duck foie gras
Sunflower oil • 1 shallot, minced • ⅓ cup white wine
3 egg yolks • 2 cups Vin Jaune • 2 cups whipped cream • 1½ ounces young Comté [AOP]
3 tablespoons Périgueux sauce (recipe not included) or chicken stock made with dry white wine

• Prepare the asparagus: Peel then blanch the asparagus in boiling water for 3 to 4 minutes until just tender; plunge into iced water to chill. Season with salt and pepper. The asparagus should still have a slight crunch. Heat two tablespoons of butter until foaming. Roll the asparagus in the butter, remove the asparagus to a baking sheet, and keep warm in the oven.

• Prepare the foie gras: Slice the foie gras into 4 thick slices and season with salt and pepper. Heat a skillet with sunflower oil until the oil is smoking, then pan sear the foie gras, basting frequently, so that the slices are golden and crisp on the outside and soft and pink in the center.

• Prepare the Vine Jaune mousseline: In a medium sauce-pan, add the minced shallot to the white wine, bring to the boil, and reduce by half. Lower the heat and add the egg yolks and two thirds of the Vin Jaune. Whisk vigorously to produce a thick, creamy zabaione-like mousse. Whisk in the clarified butter, season with salt and pepper, and pour through a fine sieve. Fold in the whipped cream and the remaining Vin Jaune.

• Preheat the broiler. On 4 ovenproof dishes, arrange 4 green asparagus and a slice of pan-seared foie gras. Cover with a thin slice of Comté and place under the broiler for several seconds to melt the cheese. Drizzle with Périgueux sauce or chicken stock and coat with the Vin Jaune mousseline sauce. Serve any remaining mousseline separately.

AMUSE-BOUCHES À LA MIMOLETTE

GÉRARD PETIT – MOF CHEESEMONGER 2004

Makes 1

1 tablespoon Mascarpone • 1 tablespoon dulce de leche (cow's or ewe's milk)
A few shavings mature, dry Mimolette

• Place the mascarpone in a small glass cup.
• Pour over the dulce de leche.

• Run the prongs of a fork across the surface of the dulce de leche and place the shavings of the Mimolette on top.

MONT D'OR AND EGG COCOTTE

FRANÇOIS BOURGON – MOF CHEESEMONGER 2011
FROMAGERIE XAVIER – TOULOUSE (DEPARTMENT 31)

Serves 4
4 slices bacon • 4 eggs • ½ round Mont d'Or ᴬᴼᴾ
Several sprigs chives, chopped
Freshly ground black pepper

• Preheat the oven to 350°F. Slice the bacon widthwise into thin strips and arrange the pieces at the bottom of 4 small ramekins set on a baking sheet.
• Separate the whites of 4 eggs, without breaking the yolks; set aside the yolks. Whip the egg whites to stiff peaks with a handheld blender or stand mixer.
• Bring water to a simmer in a medium saucepan. Cut the Mont d'Or (with rind) into small pieces and place in a bowl. Set the bowl over the simmering water. Melt the cheese until pliable, remove from the heat, and gently fold in the whipped egg whites.

• Divide this mixture among the ramekins and bake in the oven at for 10 minutes.
• Remove from the oven, and make a small well in the center of each ramekin with the back of a spoon. Carefully place an egg yolk in each well.
• Return to the oven for 1 to 2 minutes, just until the yolk warms through and the Mont d'Or mixture browns.
• Sprinkle with the chives and a grinding of black pepper.
• Serve immediately with an Alsace Riesling.

DRUNKEN MUNSTER WITH CREAM

CHRISTELLE AND CYRILLE LORHO MOF CHEESEMONGER 2007
MAISON LORHO – STRASBOURG (DEPARTMENT 67)

Serves 4
7 ounces Munster ᴬᴼᴾ, grated • ⅓ cup Marc de Gewurztraminer (pomace brandy)
⅓ cup light cream • Salt • 2 green onions or scallions with their stalks
Freshly ground black pepper • A few whole pink peppercorns

• Place the grated cheese in a medium bowl and add the Marc de Gewurztraminer. Let marinate, covered, at room temperature for 8 to 12 hours.
• Whip the cream with a handheld blender until it forms stiff peaks, then season with salt. Coat the marinated cheese with this cream.

• Mince the onions and their stalks. Sprinkle generously over the cream. Season with freshly ground black pepper and sprinkle with pink peppercorns.
• Leave to chill, covered, in the refrigerator for a few hours.
Suggestion: Serve with a Gewurztraminer *Grand Cru*.

FRANCO-SWISS FONDUE

DOMINIQUE BOUCHAIT – MOF CHEESEMONGER 2011

Serves 4
8 Ratte potatoes • 8 Vitelotte potatoes (or any firm flesh variety)
1 loaf day-old bread • 6 cloves garlic • ½ cup olive oil
7 ounces Napoléon Commingeois
7 ounces Vacherin Fribourgeois ᴬᴼᴾ
⅔ cup dry white wine
1 teaspoon cornstarch

• Preheat oven to 400°F.
• Steam the Ratte and Vitolette potatoes for 10 minutes.
• Cut the bread into cubes and toast in the oven to make croutons.
• Peel and press the garlic cloves over the olive oil; mix well. Drizzle over the hot toasted croutons and toss well.
• Finely dice the cheeses. Heat the white wine in a medium saucepan and gradually add the small cubes of cheese, whisking constantly, then add the cornstarch and continue whisking.
• Serve with the hot potatoes and the olive oil croutons.

OSSAU-IRATY NOUGAT WITH DRIED FRUITS AND BLACK CHERRY PRESERVES

LAETITIA GABORIE – MOF CHEESEMONGER 2007

Serves 6
½ cup light cream • ½ teaspoon agar
10½ ounces Ossau-Iraty ᴬᴼᴾ grated
3 ounces black cherry preserves
1 ounce chopped hazelnuts
1 ounce flaked almonds • 1 ounce crushed pistachios

• Pour the light cream into a small saucepan and bring to the boil. Stir in the agar and simmer for 2 to 3 minutes.
• Add the grated Ossau-Iraty and stir it into the simmering cream with a spatula. When the cheese has melted, pour it into a baking dish and let cool.
• Melt the black cherry preserves in a small saucepan over a low heat. Brush the preserves over the cooled cheese.
• Sprinkle the cheese with the hazelnuts, almonds, and pistachios.
• Cut the cheese into small 1 x 1½-inch rectangles.
Suggestion: Serve as an appetizer with a white Jurançon wine.

TURNIP VELOUTÉ WITH SAINT-NECTAIRE

LAURENT DEL ARBRE – MOF CHEF 2004

Serves 4

12½ ounces round turnips

1 ounce unsalted butter

1½ ounces shallots, minced

Salt and freshly ground black pepper

2½ tablespoons white stock

7 ounces Saint-Nectaire [AOP], rind removed

• Peel and chop the turnips into chunks. Reserve 2 ounces of the turnips for a garnish. Place the butter in a medium saucepan set over medium heat, add the minced shallots, and sweat for 5 minutes.

• Add the turnips, except those reserved for the garnish. Season with salt and pepper and moisten with the white stock. Let cook for 20 minutes. Blend the shallots, turnips, and stock with the Saint-Nectaire. Adjust the seasoning, if necessary.

• Finely dice a portion of the reserved turnip and finely slice the rest. Serve in bowls and sprinkle with the diced turnip and turnip slices on top.

ROQUEFORT AND COTEAUX-DU-LAYON WITH POACHED PEARS AND DARK CHOCOLATE

MICHEL FOUCHEREAU – MOF CHEESEMONGER 2004

Serves 4

17½ ounces Roquefort AOP • ¾ cup Coteaux-du-Layon (sweet white wine)

2 ripe pears • 2 cups poaching syrup (see Note)

4 squares 100% cocoa dark chocolate • Chilled pear liqueur • Ice

• In a medium bowl, mix the Roquefort and Coteaux-du-Layon with a wooden spoon to form a smooth paste; refrigerate.

• Cut the pears in half, remove the core, and poach the pears until tender in the poaching syrup .

• Let cool and then finely slice the poached pear halves lengthwise.

• Grate the chocolate into a bowl.

• Into wide ramekins, spoon in a base of the Roquefort paste, fan out slices of poached pear on top, and cover with the grated chocolate.

• Serve as a dessert at room temperature with a small glass of chilled pear liqueur over ice.

Note: To make 2 cups poaching syrup, dissolve 1 cup cane sugar or honey in 2 cups water in a small saucepan over low heat.

PÉLARDON, PARMA HAM, AND FRESH FIG DÉLICES

MARIE QUATREHOMME – MOF CHEESEMONGER 2000
FROMAGERIE QUATREHOMME – PARIS (DEPARTMENT 75)

Makes 32 tartlets
9 ounces shortcrust pastry (use your favorite recipe)
8 thin slices Parma ham • 4 rounds Pélardon [AOP]
8 small fresh figs
8 teaspoons acacia honey
Freshly ground black pepper

• Preheat the oven to 350°F.
• Roll out the shortcrust pastry. Using a cookie cutter, or a glass with a similar diameter to your mini-tart pans, cut 32 small rounds of pastry and place them in the molds of the pans.
• Prick the pastry rounds with a fork and place dry beans on the top. Blind bake in the oven for 10 minutes to brown the rounds slightly. Remove the beans and set aside the pans.

• Trim the fat off the ham, then cut each slice into four and roll each small quarter slice into a roll.
• Cut each Pélardon into 8 slices; quarter the figs. Place a piece of ham and cheese, and a fig quarter, onto the tart base. Drizzle honey over each tartlet and sprinkle with finely ground black pepper.
• Preheat the broiler. Place the pans under the broiler for 3 minutes, watching carefully so the tartlets do not burn. Serve warm.

ZUCCHINI GRATIN WITH RAVIOLES DU DAUPHINÉ

DOMINIQUE BOUCHAIT – MOF CHEESEMONGER 2011

Serves 4
4¼ cups light cream • Salt • Pepper • 3 garlic cloves, crushed
Grated nutmeg • 4 zucchini • 8 sheets Emmental Ravioles du Dauphiné (or substitute mini cheese-filled ravioli and place several in each layer) • Emmental, grated

• Preheat the oven to 400°F.
• Pour the light cream into a salad bowl, and season with salt and pepper. Add the crushed garlic and a sprinkling of grated nutmeg.
• Slice the zucchini into matchsticks and arrange a layer on the bottom of a baking dish, then place a sheet of Ravioles du Dauphiné and another layer of zucchini. Coat with some of the cream mixture.
• Continue layering the ravioli, zucchini, and cream (you will create 8 layers total), finishing with a layer of cream. Bake in the oven for 30 minutes, then sprinkle over the grated Emmental. Return to the oven for 5 minutes until the cheese is golden. Serve hot.

BANANA AND ROQUEFORT GRATIN

XAVIER THURET – MOF CHEESEMONGER 2007

Serves 4

1 tablespoon salted butter • 2 bananas
5½ ounces Roquefort Baragnaudes [AOP]
5½ ounces crumbled Speculoos or spiced shortcrust cookies

• Butter a small baking dish with the butter. Slice the banana and lay the slices on the bottom of the dish.
• Crush the Roquefort with a fork and sprinkle over the bananas. Top with a thick layer of the crumbled cookies.

• Preheat the broiler and set the dish in the oven. Broil until the cookie crust browns. Watch carefully so it doesn't burn.
Suggestion: Serve with a glass of aged amber rum.

CAPPUCCINO OF SAINT-MARCELLIN WITH CAVIAR

BERNARD MURE-RAVAUD – MOF CHEESEMONGER 2007
FROMAGERIE DES ALPAGES – GRENOBLE (DEPARTMENT 38)

Serves 4

7 ounces Vitelotte potatoes
5½ tablespoons unsalted butter
Salt
Freshly ground black pepper
2 rounds mature Saint-Marcellin [AOP]
½ cup heavy whipping cream
1½ ounces caviar

• Peel the potatoes and cook in a saucepan of boiling water. When cooked through, drain and mash the potatoes and stir in the butter. Adjust the seasoning and keep warm.
• Blend together the cheese and cream in a food processor until light and frothy. Season with salt and pep-

per. Pour the mixture into a whipping siphon, seal, shake vigorously, and place in the refrigerator.
• Just before serving, fill 4 small cups halfway with potato. Cover with the Saint-Marcellin cream and add a large spoon of caviar. Serve immediately.

STUFFED CUCUMBERS
WITH ROQUEFORT CREAM AND PARMESAN TUILES

CHRISTIAN JANIER – MOF CHEESEMONGER 2000

Serves 4

1 cucumber (2 to 2.5 inches thick)

Coarse sea salt

5½ ounces Roquefort AOP

1 cup light cream

⅓ cup port (optional)

Grated nutmeg

Salt

Freshly ground black pepper

3½ ounces Parmigiano Reggiano, finely grated

Poppy seeds (optional)

Olive oil

Balsamic vinegar

Lamb's lettuce

Arugula lettuce

Cherry tomatoes

• Prepare the cucumbers: Peel the cucumber in alternate strips, slice it in half lengthwise, scoop out the seeds with a small teaspoon, and cut into 8 to 12 pieces with a crinkle-cutter. Sprinkle with coarse sea salt and set aside for a few minutes to drain the excess moisture.

• Prepare the stuffing: Cream together the Roquefort, cream, and a tablespoon of port, if using, to obtain a smooth paste. Add a pinch of grated nutmeg and season with salt and pepper.

• Using a pastry bag, pipe stuffing onto the cucumber sections and refrigerate.

• Prepare the Parmesan tuiles: If using poppy seeds, add them to the grated cheese. Lay a sheet of parchment paper on a nonstick baking sheet. Place 3-inch-wide ring molds on top. Spoon the grated cheese into the molds to form a thin round of grated cheese. Remove the molds; repeat to make more rounds of cheese.

• Preheat the broiler. Toast under the broiler until golden, 2 to 3 minutes. Carefully peel the tuiles from the parchment paper (watch out they are hot!) and cool on a rolling pin to give them a curved shape.

• Prepare a vinaigrette by combining the olive oil, vinegar, salt, and pepper.

• To serve: Start with a bed of lamb's lettuce and arugula, and drizzle with the vinaigrette. Place 2 or 3 pieces of stuffed cucumber on top, along with a Parmesan tuile. Decorate with cherry tomatoes to add a touch of color.

RAVIOLI NAPOLÉON

BERNARD LEPRINCE – MOF CHEF 1996

Serves 4
1 cup flour
1 egg • Olive oil
17 ounces Napoléon Commingeois
11 tablespoons (⅔ cup) butter
2 ounces shallot, minced
½ cup white wine (e.g. Tariquet)
1 cup white stock
Salt, Freshly ground black pepper
1 sprig sage
1 clove garlic
Espelette pepper (optional)
1 tablespoon olive oil

• Prepare the ravioli pasta: In a medium bowl, mix together the flour and egg to obtain a firm dough. Knead the dough until smooth. Lightly massage with olive oil and place in a resealable plastic bag in the refrigerator for one hour.

• Prepare the ravioli: Cut the Napoléon cheese into small pieces. Using a rolling pin, or pasta machine, roll out the ravioli pasta into a thin sheet. Let rest for 15 minutes. With a 3-inch-diameter cookie cutter, cut out 24 circles. Place a small teaspoon of Napoléon cheese on the circle. Using a brush, moisten the edges of the ravioli with water and fold in two, pressing down the edges. Set aside.

• Prepare the white wine sauce: In a medium saucepan, heat 2 tablespoons butter until it begins to turn nut brown, then sweat the minced shallots without browning them. Deglaze with the white wine. Add the white stock, bring to the boil, and simmer to reduce by half. Vigorously whip in the remaining butter, season with salt and pepper and add the sage. Keep warm.

• In a large pot of boiling salted water, add the garlic and a tablespoon of olive oil. Cook the ravioli for 4 minutes, then drain.

• Divide the ravioli among four shallow dishes. Strain the sauce through a fine sieve (to remove the shallot and sage). Add finely ground black pepper, or Espelette pepper, and serve.

Seasonal suggestions: In the fall, add porcini to the stuffing; in winter, truffle; in spring, morel mushrooms; in summer, peas.

Other recipes

BLEU D'AUVERGNE AND WALNUT CAKE

Serves 6

1½ cups flour, plus extra for the pan

2 teaspoons baking powder

3 eggs • ⅓ cup milk

⅓ cup walnut oil

Salt, Freshly ground black pepper

1 apple (Reinette or similar can be used), peeled, cored, and cut into eighths

5½ ounces Bleu d'Auvergne [AOP]

3½ oz ounces grated Emmental

2 ounces walnuts

1 tablespoon butter for the dish

• Preheat the oven to 350°F.

• In a large bowl, mix together the flour and baking powder and form a well in the middle.

• In a small bowl, beat together the eggs, the milk, and the oil, and add a pinch of salt and pepper. Pour this mixture into the well in the middle of the flour and gradually incorporate into the flour.

• When the mixture is smooth, add the apple, crumble in the Bleu d'Auvergne, the grated Emmental, and the walnuts.

• Butter and flour an 11-inch cake pan and pour in the mixture. Bake in the oven for 40 minutes; a toothpick inserted in the center should come out clean. Remove the pan from the oven, let cool slightly, then unmold and leave the cake to cool completely.

BERTHOUD

Serves 4

2 cloves garlic

17½ ounces Abondance [AOP]

Salt • Freshly ground black pepper

2½ tablespoons white wine (ideally a Savoie white)

2½ tablespoons Madeira

- Preheat the broiler.
- Peel 1 clove of garlic and crush it lightly with the flat of a large knife. Rub it around the bottom of 4 small ramekins and discard.
- Mince the remaining garlic and divide it among the ramekins. Slice the Abondance into thin strips and divide them equally among the ramekins.
- Add a pinch of salt and sprinkle generously with black pepper. Pour the white wine and Madeira over each ramekin. Place under the broiler for 6 to 8 minutes, until golden.

FONDUE SAVOYARDE (A VARIATION)

Serves 6

1 loaf crusty bread

17½ ounces Beaufort [AOP]

14 ounces Comté [AOP]

11 ounces Tomme de Savoie

1 teaspoon cornstarch

1 ounce kirsch • 1 clove garlic

2 glasses (or 10 ounces) dry white wine

¼ round Reblochon [AOP]

- Cut the bread into cubes and set aside to dry slightly.
- Remove the rind from the Beaufort, Comté, and Tomme de Savoie. Cut the cheeses into thin slices.
- Mix the cornstarch into the kirsch until it dissolves.
- Lightly crush the garlic with the flat of a knife and rub the bottom of the fondue pot; discard the garlic.
- In the fondue pot, heat the white wine on medium until simmering. Reduce the heat and gradually add the slices of cheese, stirring regularly with a wooden spoon in a figure-eight movement. When the cheeses have melted, add the Reblochon. Stir in the kirsch-cornstarch thickener.
- Place the fondue dish on the fondue burner and stir from time to time with a wooden spoon. Use fondue or other long forks to dip the bread cubes into the fondue.

BRIE DE MELUN QUICHE

Serves 6

1 roll shortcrust pastry • 2 tablespoons unsalted butter
1 onion, minced • 3 eggs
½ cup crème fraîche
Salt • Freshly ground black pepper
3½ ounces Brie de Melun ^{AOP}

• Preheat the oven to 400°F.
• Lay the shortcrust pastry into a shallow 8-inch pie plate and prick the pastry with a fork.
• Heat the butter in a small saucepan over low heat. When the butter begins to froth, add the minced onion and fry until golden.

• Beat the eggs and crème fraîche in a bowl, season with salt and pepper, and add the fried onion.
• Dice the Brie de Melun and sprinkle evenly over the pastry, then pour the egg–crème fraîche mixture on top. Bake in the oven for 30 minutes.

CAMEMBERT DE NORMANDIE AND APPLE FEUILLETÉ

Serves 4

3 Granny Smith apples
1 Camembert de Normandie ^{AOP}
1 10 x 15 sheet puff pastry
1 egg yolk, beaten

• Preheat the oven to 400°F. Line a baking sheet with parchment paper.
• Peel and core the apples, and cut them into small cubes.
• Cut the Camembert de Normandie into strips.
• Gently roll out the sheet of puff pastry and cut it in half. Take one of the pieces of puff pastry and place four small piles of apples equally spaced along its length and lay the strips of Camembert on top. Cover with the second piece of puff pastry and gently press the pastry around the piles of cheese and apple.

• Cut the pastry into four and seal the edges of the pies. Place the pastries on the prepared baking sheet and brush the tops with egg yolk.
• Place the pan in the oven and bake until golden, 20 to 25 minutes.

CANTAL TRUFFADE

Serves 6

2 pounds 3 ounces firm potatoes

2 cloves garlic, crushed • Grapeseed oil

Salt, Freshly ground black pepper

7 ounces smoked bacon, cut into thin strips

17½ ounces fresh Tomme du Cantal

17½ ounces Cantal *jeune* ^{AOP} • 3 tablespoons crème fraîche

• Peel the potatoes, cut them into rounds, and steam until tender, about 20 minutes. Drain the potatoes.

• Place the garlic in a medium sauté pan with a little oil, then add the potatoes and fry over medium heat for 10 minutes. Season with salt and pepper. Add the strips of smoked bacon and fry for a further 5 minutes.

• Dice the Tomme and Cantal. Add the cheese to the potato-bacon mixture and stir for 5 to 10 minutes. Add the crème fraîche and stir together until the melting cheese binds the mixture together. Serve immediately.

CHAMPENOISE TOMATOES

Serves 6

6 red beefsteak tomatoes

1 onion • 1 tablespoon unsalted butter

17½ ounces bacon, cut into thin strips

Salt, Freshly ground black pepper

1 heaping tablespoon crème fraîche

Several sprigs cilantro • 1 Chaource ^{AOP}

3 teaspoons Espelette pepper jelly • Olive oil

• Preheat the oven to 350°F. Line a baking sheet with parchment paper.

• Slice the tops off the tomatoes and scoop out the pulp; reserve the tops and pulp. Sprinkle the hollow tomatoes with salt and turn them upside down on a rack to drain the juice. Set aside.

• Peel the onion and mince in a food processor. Fry the minced onion in the butter. Add the tomato pulp and cook until the water evaporates.

• Fry the bacon separately. Add the cooked tomato pulp and lightly season with salt and pepper. Add the crème fraîche and stir. Add the chopped cilantro.

• Place the hollow tomatoes on the prepared baking sheet. Cut the Chaource into 12 slices. Place one slice on the bottom of each tomato. Add a ½ teaspoon of Espelette pepper jelly per tomato. Fill the tomatoes with the bacon-tomato mixture, add another slice of cheese, and place the tops on each stuffed tomato. Drizzle the tomatoes with olive oil.

• Place in the oven for 20 minutes, then serve hot.

PORCINI MUSHROOM OMELET WITH COMTÉ

Serves 1

3 ripe tomatoes

3 tablespoons olive oil

4 or 5 basil leaves

Salt • Freshly ground black pepper

½ slice fresh bread

1 clove garlic

½ bunch parsley

2 ounces Comté ^{AOP}, plus extra for shaving • 3 eggs

2 ounces porcini mushrooms

• Peel the tomatoes, then cut them in half and scoop out the seeds. Mince the tomato flesh in a food processor and add the olive oil and basil leaves, process further; season with salt and pepper. Place the tomato mixture on the bread.

• Mince the garlic and parsley in a food processor. Gently heat a splash of olive oil in a small sauté pan, and fry the garlic and parsley.

• Grate the Comté. Beat the eggs in a small bowl and add the grated Comté.

• In a small nonstick sauté pan coated with olive oil, fry the porcini mushrooms over high heat. Season with salt and add the garlic and parsley. Pour in the egg-cheese mixture and cook for several minutes. Fold the omelet over and serve hot.

• Sprinkle the omelet with a few fine shavings of Comté and serve the tomato toast alongside.

HOT POTATOES WITH ÉPOISSES

Serves 4

6 firm-flesh potatoes (such as red bliss or new potatoes)

3½ ounces Epoisses ^{AOP} • 2 ounces sorrel, peeled

½ cup light cream

Salt, Freshly ground black pepper

Coarse sea salt

• Cook the potatoes until tender in a saucepan of salted water. Drain the potatoes and halve or quarter them when cool enough to handle.

• Cut the cheese into 8 slices. Finely chop the sorrel. Whip the cream to soft peaks with a handheld blender and fold in the chopped sorrel. Season gene-rously with salt and pepper.

• Place a layer of the sorrel mixture on 4 plates and arrange the halved or quartered potatoes on top. Place two slices of cheese on top of the potatoes and sprinkle with coarse sea salt and coarsely ground black pepper.

GRATIN OF FRESH PASTA WITH CREAMY MUSHROOM SAUCE AND FOURME D'AMBERT

Serves 4

1 pound long, fresh pasta • 2 tablespoons unsalted butter

7 ounces oyster or chanterelle mushrooms

1 shallot, minced

2 ounces black Bigorre ham (or dried, cured mountain ham), diced

¾ cup dry white wine • Several sprigs parsley

1½ cups light cream • Salt • Freshly ground black pepper

4 slices Fourme d'Ambert AOP

• Cook the fresh pasta according to the package directions, then toss with 1 tablespoon of the butter. Set aside.

• Prepare the creamy mushroom sauce: Gently fry the oyster or chanterelle mushrooms in a sauté pan with the remaining butter. In another pan, fry the minced shallot with the diced ham; add the mushrooms. Stir well and add the white wine. Cook to allow the liquid to reduce, then add the chopped parsley and light cream. Season with salt and pepper.

• Divide the cooked pasta among 4 ovenproof stoneware bowls. Add 2 tablespoons of creamy mushroom sauce to each. Top with a slice of Fourme d'Ambert.

• Preheat the broiler. Place the bowls under the broiler on a baking sheet to brown the cheese.

SALAD OF BLACKBERRIES, APPLE, AND FOURME D'AMBERT

Serves 4

1 head lettuce or baby spinach • 2 tablespoons pine nuts

5 tablespoons walnut oil • 2 tablespoons cider vinegar

Salt, Freshly ground black pepper

2 Granny Smith apples • 2 Gala apples

7 ounces Fourme d'Ambert AOP

20 blackberries • 4 slices crusty white bread, lightly toasted

• Wash and drain the lettuce. Toast the pine nuts in a hot pan.

• Prepare a vinaigrette with oil, vinegar, salt, and pepper.

• Cut the apples into thin slices. Arrange the apple slices on 4 plates, alternating the types of apple.

• Thinly slice the Fourme d'Ambert and place slices of cheese between the slices of apple. Arrange lettuce leaves, toasted pine nuts, and fresh blackberries around the apples and cheese. Drizzle with vinaigrette.

• Serve with the toast.

MAROILLES FLAMICHE

Serves 4

3½ teaspoons bread yeast • ¼ cup warm milk
7 tablespoons unsalted butter, softened, plus more for greasing
7 ounces flour • 2 eggs • Salt
14 ounces Maroilles ᴬᴼᴾ
Freshly ground black pepper
2 tablespoons crème fraîche

• Mix the yeast into the milk and soften the butter in the milk and yeast. Mix the flour and eggs together with a little salt, and then mix in the milk and yeast. Knead the dough on a floured work surface until smooth and elastic.
• Remove the rind from the Maroilles, and slice it thinly. Season with pepper. Grease a shallow 8-inch pie plate.
• Roll out the dough into a 12-inch-diameter circle.

Place in the prepared pie plate. Lay the slices of cheese on the dough and leave the dough to rise at room temperature for approximately 1 hour.
• Preheat the oven to 350°F.
• Season the crème fraîche with salt and pepper and spread over the dough. Bake in the oven for 30 minutes. Stick a knife in the pie and make sure it comes out clean to indicate doneness. Serve hot.

MORTEAU SAUSAGE WITH MONT D'OR-POTATO GRATIN

Serves 4

2 Morteau sausages
4 Charlotte potatoes • ⅓ cup milk
1¾ cups crème fraîche
7 ounces Mont d'Or ᴬᴼᴾ
1 teaspoon potato starch
Salt • Freshly ground pepper • 4 egg yolks • Chervil

• Cook the sausages in water for 30 minutes; remove and cut into slices.
• Cook the potatoes and slice them diagonally.
• In a saucepan, stir together the milk, crème fraîche, and Mont d'Or, and bring to a boil. Stir in the potato starch. Season with salt and pepper, remove from the heat, and let cool. Add the egg yolks and whip the mixture with a whisk to create a smooth, creamy sauce.

• Place 4 medium ramekins on a baking sheet. Arrange the slices of sausage and potato in each ramekin and top with the Mont d'Or cream.
• Preheat the broiler. Place the baking sheet in the oven and broil for 5 minutes to brown the cream. Serve hot with a sprig of chervil.

NEUFCHÂTEL SOUFFLÉ

Serves 6
7 tablespoons butter • 1 cup flour
4¼ cups milk • 5 eggs separated
7 ounces Neufchâtel ᴬᴼᴾ • Salt
Freshly ground black pepper • Nutmeg

• Preheat the oven to 300°F.
• Prepare the béchamel sauce: Melt the butter in a medium saucepan over a low heat, add the flour, and stir for 1 minute. Gradually add the milk and stir vigorously to combine with the flour and butter. Remove from the heat and stir in the 5 egg yolks. With a handheld blender or stand mixer, beat the egg whites to form stiff peaks.
• Crush the Neufchâtel with a fork and stir into the béchamel sauce preparation. Using a spatula, carefully fold the beaten egg whites into the Neufchâtel sauce and season with salt and pepper.
• Pour the mixture into a buttered and floured 8-inch soufflé dish. Bake for 30 to 35 minutes, then increase the temperature to 350°F for 10 minutes. Avoid the temptation to open the oven door before the end of the cooking time or your soufflé might collapse.

TARTIFLETTE

Serves 4
2¼ pounds firm-flesh potatoes
Olive oil
7 ounces onion, minced
7 ounces smoked bacon, cut into strips
1 soft, ripe Reblochon ᴬᴼᴾ
1 clove garlic, crushed

• Preheat the oven to 400°F.
• Rinse, dry, peel, and dice the potatoes.
• Heat a little oil in a saucepan and sweat the onions. Add the potatoes, and fry until they begin to brown. Add the bacon and finish cooking, until potatoes are tender and bacon is crispy.
• Scrape the rind of the Reblochon completely off with the blade of a knife. Cut the cheese in half horizontally, then quarter each half.
• Rub the base of a 12-inch gratin dish with garlic.
• Spoon half of the potatoes and bacon in the dish. Arrange four pieces of Reblochon on top, then place the remaining potatoes and bacon over the cheese. Finish with the remainder of the Reblochon, rind face down on the potatoes. Bake in the oven for about 15 minutes. If desired, crisp the tartiflette by placing it under the broiler for 5 minutes.

SWEET POTATO ALIGOT

Serves 6

2 pounds 10 ounces sweet potatoes • ⅔ cup single cream
Salt, Freshly ground black pepper • 7 ounces Salers AOP, finely diced
2 ounces Napoléon Commingeois, grated

• Peel the sweet potatoes and cut them into chunks. Boil a pot of water, plunge in the sweet potato chunks, and boil for 10 minutes. Drain and purée in a food processor, while gradually pouring in the single cream. Season with salt and pepper.

• Stir the diced Salers into the creamy sweet potato purée and stir well.

• Preheat the broiler. Place 4 medium ramekins on a baking sheet. Fill the ramekins with the purée, top with the grated Napoléon Commingeois, and broil until golden.

VALENÇAY SOUP WITH HAZELNUTS

Serves 4

1 small shallot • 4 tablespoons olive oil
7 ounces ripe tomatoes
Salt • Freshly ground black pepper
1 tablespoon tomato paste
9 ounces Valençay AOP • 1½ cups whole milk
6 ounces leg of lamb • ½ ounce hazelnuts • 1 egg yolk

• Prepare a coulis: Mince the shallot, then heat 2 tablespoons olive oil in a saucepan and sweat the shallot for 2 minutes without letting it brown. Cut the tomatoes into chunks and add to the shallots. Season with salt and pepper. Cook on low heat for 30 minutes, then add the tomato paste and stir to combine. Blend in the food processor, then strain through a fine sieve and adjust the seasoning.

• While the coulis is cooking, scrape the rind of the Valençay off completely and cut the cheese into pieces. Place in a medium saucepan, cover with the milk, and heat on low, stirring from time to time. When the cheese has melted, blend the mixture in a food processor to make a soup; season with salt and pepper.

• Cut the leg of lamb into tiny cubes.

• Brown the hazelnuts in a saucepan, crush them, and set aside 1 teaspoon for the garnish.

• Mix together the lamb cubes, the remainder of the hazelnuts, and the egg yolk. Season with salt and pepper and form the mixture into twenty small, thin patties. Heat 2 tablespoons olive oil in a sauté pan over medium-high heat and cook the lamb patties for one minute on each side.

• Divide the patties among 4 warmed soup dishes, top with soup, dollop with tomato coulis, and sprinkle with the reserved crushed hazelnuts.

INDEX

* The numbers in bold refer to the detailed recipes in this book.

ACKNOWLEDGMENTS

I'd especially like to thank Coralie Fourcadet-Vaz, Adeline Paraud, and Delphine Kopff Hausser. Thank you, Coralie, for coordinating and compiling the team's answers and for your meticulous research in making this book possible. I knew I could count on you to bring it all together and write it in your marvelous style. Thank you, Adeline, for your invaluable editing work, painstakingly checking dates and data, often in your free time. I knew I could count on you. Thank you, Delphine, for your writing. I know I'm always easy to "adapt" into words. I am eternally grateful to all three of you for your great patience through this adventure. Without you, this book would never have become what it is!!! Our business would not exist without the team-work and permanent consultation that bind us together. In every adventure I undertake, my dedicated team is always right behind me: thank you, then, Sylvie Abadie, Jérémy De Almeida, Robin De Almeida, Thomas De Almeida, Antoine Bouchait, Corine Boucheron, Sophie Canut, Pascal Cappelle, Françoise Cougrand, Anne Dubary, Jennifer Dumoret, Christiane Duplan, Nelly Duplan, Adèle Dupuy, Dominique Encausse, Célia Lam-raoui, Nathalie Matignon, Aline Mazana, Caroline Palu, Marjorie Pratviel, Christine Rodriguez, Annick San-guin, and Ana Tavarez. You have all contributed in your own precious ways, and I am very grateful to you. I would also like to thank my editor, Laurence Lehoux, for her patience, her compassion, the partnership she has built, and her commitment to this work. Finally I wish to thank the photographer, Marie-Pierre Morel, who has managed to capture these wonderful cheeses with such elegance and grace.

A huge thank you to all of you.
DOMINIQUE BOUCHAIT

First published in the United States of America in 2019 by
Rizzoli International Publications, Inc.
300 Park Avenue South
New York, NY 10010
www.rizzoliusa.com

Originally published in French in 2016 under the title, *Fromages, Le Bon Goût du Terroir*
by Éditions du Chêne

© 2016, Éditions du Chêne – Hachette Livre
Photography: © Marie-Pierre Morel

General director: Fabienne Kriegel
Chief editor: Laurence Lehoux
Proofreading: Valérie Mettais, Valérie Nigdelian
Editorial assistant: Suzy Cacheux
Content manager: Delphine Hausser
Artistic direction: Sabine Houplain assisted by Élodie Palumbo
Graphic design and production: Marie-Paule Jaulme
Cover typography: Yann Le Dluz
Drawing, cartography: Marion Vandenbroucke
Production: Nicole Thiériot-Pichon
Photoengraving: Quat'coul
Translation : Jonno Slysa
Partnerships and direct sales: Mathilde Barrois mbarrois@hachette-livre.fr
Press relations: Hélène Maurice hmaurice@hachette-livre.fr

2019 2020 2021 2022 / 10 9 8 7 6 5 4 3 2 1
ISBN: 978-0-8478-6673-1
Library of Congress Control Number: 2018957529

Printed in China